Praise for *The Easy Bible...*

Having taught Bible study methods at Moody Bible Institute for over twenty-five years, I can confidently say that *The Easy Bible Study Method* is a remarkable achievement. This book distills complex principles into an accessible framework that is both practical and profound. Ashley, Taylor, and Ellen expertly balance depth with clarity, making Bible study attainable for all believers. I especially appreciate how they weave personal stories with solid teaching, making Bible study feel accessible rather than overwhelming. This book doesn't just teach you how to study Scripture; it inspires you to fall in love with God's Word for yourself.

Jim Coakley
Professor of Bible, Moody Bible Institute; author of *14 Fresh Ways to Enjoy the Bible*

I *loved* this book. *The Easy Bible Study Method* is one of the most joy-filled, practical, and theologically rich guides to studying Scripture I've ever read. Ellen, Ashley, and Taylor have created something truly special—an invitation to stop striving and start delighting in God's Word. This book will make you want to open your Bible again and again, not out of obligation, but out of sheer joy.

Jordan Raynor
Bestselling author of *The Sacredness of Secular Work* and *Redeeming Your Time*

Whether you're new to the Bible or you've been reading it your whole life, *The Easy Bible Study Method* can help you develop consistent rhythms as you study Scripture. In this book, Ashley, Taylor, and Ellen have created a valuable resource that will help you dig deeper into God's Word and apply it to your life.

Tim Wildsmith
Author of *Bible Translations for Everyone* and *Daily Scripture Guidebook*

The Easy Bible Study Method is a solid resource for anyone just getting started with Bible study or looking to take their Bible study deeper. Ashley, Taylor, and Ellen lay everything out in a clear, step-by-step way that makes studying Scripture feel a lot less intimidating. It's straightforward, practical, and encouraging—perfect for building confidence in your Bible studies and helping you form strong Bible study habits from the ground up.

Faith Womack
Bible study educator and content creator

THE EASY

A GUIDE TO UNDERSTANDING, APPLYING, AND DELIGHTING IN GOD'S WORD

BIBLE STUDY METHOD

ASHLEY ARMIJO, TAYLOR KRAUSE & ELLEN KRAUSE

The Creators of *Coffee and Bible Time*

Moody Publishers

CHICAGO

© 2024 by
ASHLEY ARMIJO, TAYLOR KRAUSE, AND ELLEN KRAUSE

All rights reserved. No part of this book may be reproduced in any form without permission in writing from the publisher, except in the case of brief quotations embodied in critical articles or reviews.

Scripture quotations are from the ESV® Bible (The Holy Bible, English Standard Version®), © 2001 by Crossway, a publishing ministry of Good News Publishers. Used by permission. All rights reserved. The ESV text may not be quoted in any publication made available to the public by a Creative Commons license. The ESV may not be translated in whole or in part into any other language.

Scripture quotations marked (NIV) are taken from the Holy Bible, New International Version®, NIV®. Copyright © 1973, 1978, 1984, 2011 by Biblica, Inc.™ Used by permission of Zondervan. All rights reserved worldwide. www.zondervan.com The "NIV" and "New International Version" are trademarks registered in the United States Patent and Trademark Office by Biblica, Inc.™

Scripture quotations marked (NLT) are taken from the *Holy Bible*, New Living Translation, copyright ©1996, 2004, 2015 by Tyndale House Foundation. Used by permission of Tyndale House Publishers, Carol Stream, Illinois 60188. All rights reserved.

Edited by Ashleigh Slater
Interior design: Puckett Smartt
Cover design: Brittany Schrock
Authors photo: Isaac Mitchell

ISBN: 978-0-8024-3419-7

Originally delivered by fleets of horse-drawn wagons, the affordable paperbacks from D. L. Moody's publishing house resourced the church and served everyday people. Now, after more than 125 years of publishing and ministry, Moody Publishers' mission remains the same—even if our delivery systems have changed a bit. For more information on other books (and resources) created from a biblical perspective, go to www.moodypublishers.com or write to:

Moody Publishers
820 N. LaSalle Boulevard
Chicago, IL 60610

1 3 5 7 9 10 8 6 4 2

Printed in Colombia

For our beloved Coffee and Bible Time community—
thank you for walking this journey with us

Contents

Before Diving In 9

The Journey Begins 11

What to Expect 15

1. E—Enter into the Story 19

2. A—Assess the Main Idea 63

3. S—Seek God and His Character 95

4. Y—Yearn for a Heart Change and Deeper Intimacy with God 113

5. Putting It All Together 133

Conclusion 167

A Note to Mentors 173

Appendix A: John 6:1–15 177

Appendix B: Recommended Resources 178

Appendix C: EASY Bible Study Method Guides 180

Appendix D: Map 185

Acknowledgments 186

Before Diving In

From Ashley, Taylor, and Mentor Mama Ellen

Before we dive deep into Bible study, we want to introduce ourselves! This book comes from the hearts of two sisters, Ashley and Taylor, and our mom, Ellen. The three of us do online ministry together and love connecting with people all over the world and teaching them how to study the Bible.

While this book will teach you our EASY Bible Study Method, studying Scripture has not always come "easy" to us. We remember what it felt like to open the first page of the Bible and question if

Welcome

Scan to get to know us, or go to:

coffeeandbibletime.com

we had what it takes to read through the whole thing. We remember Bible study days when we were left with more questions than answers. And we remember what it felt like to wonder if all this hard work of study was worth it. But by the grace of God, we didn't let discouragement keep us from reading! Little by little, year by year, we learned how to study the Bible. We grew in our faith tremendously as we consistently pursued God through the pages of Scripture. To this day, we continue exploring the depths of God's Word, learning, growing, and actively pursuing Jesus.

THE EASY BIBLE STUDY METHOD

Our favorite moments are spent with a hot mug of coffee and our Bibles flipped open to read and highlight. When you taste and see just how sweet God's Word is, you will find your favorite moments are spent in Scripture too!

We are so excited that you desire to study the Bible and have joined us in this pursuit. Let's get started!

The Journey Begins

From Ashley

Have you ever felt so overwhelmed and exhausted that you couldn't catch your breath? That was me in college. I was knee-deep academically, working toward my undergrad degree in biblical studies at the Moody Bible Institute in downtown Chicago. I was also on a "hamster wheel" of commitments outside my classwork. For months, I said yes to every social and academic opportunity offered to me and ignored the signs that my emotional, mental, and social batteries were running dangerously low. I couldn't catch my breath, to say the least.

When the world shut down due to the unexpected worldwide pandemic, I finally had time to take a deep breath. But when I stopped, I crashed hard, like I had been running at full speed toward a brick wall. When the shock wore off and the stillness and silence finally set in, I realized it was the wake-up call I needed.

Being forced to slow down gave me time to reflect on where I was actually at: burnt out, stressed, anxious, and overwhelmed. I was a mess, but I knew that **God is not afraid of our messes; He takes pleasure in embracing us exactly where we are.** In my weakness, I turned to God, and He met me in my deepest needs. Quarantine became a new opportunity for me to seek God on a deeper level through prayer and Bible study. I took full advantage of the hours I could spend with Him.

During this time, God refilled my empty cup. The still and quiet moments I had at Jesus' feet refreshed my soul and inspired me creatively. Taylor, our mom, and I came together to create content for our online ministry, Coffee and Bible Time. Our goal was to help hundreds of thousands of women worldwide come to know Jesus in a deeper way through Bible study.

One sunny spring morning, I sat at my desk with the windows cracked open and my coffee-stained Bible on my lap. I opened up my journal to a fresh page that was ready to receive all the creative ideas that had been brewing in my head. I was reflecting on our online community's needs, specifically, their struggle to read and understand Scripture. My heart was filled with compassion, and I deeply desired to create a tool to help them get into God's Word and experience it like I had. I scribbled down my thoughts fast and furiously, which is how the EASY Bible Study Method was born.

After creating and refining the EASY Bible Study Method, we shared it on YouTube. It quickly became our number one downloaded resource. Not only have we seen our online community thrive using this method, but we have introduced it to friends, mentees, and small groups, and have been blown away at how this tool has helped them learn how to study the Bible in a deeper and more personal way.

What about you? What brought you to this book? Perhaps you've had some of these thoughts when attempting to read the Bible before:

I don't understand what's going on.
Where do I begin?
I get bored too fast.
I feel overwhelmed.
I'll get to it later.
I don't have the time.

If that's you, I promise you are not alone in your thoughts. We have been there too. The EASY Bible Study Method was created so you can finally overcome those roadblocks and give Bible study a new and fresh go!

And friend, since you are reading this book, I know there is a desire within

The Journey Begins

you to get into God's Word! It is God who gives you a heart to know Him (Jer. 24:7). He transforms us through the Holy Spirit to know Him and understand truth (Phil. 2:13; John 16:13). The desire you have to read Scripture is ultimately from Him because He loves you and wants a relationship with you. (How incredible is that!) It is my prayer that your hunger and thirst for God's Word (1 Peter 2:2–3) will only continue to grow. That you may taste and see through the pages of Scripture that He is so good (Ps. 34:8) and long to return to it as your daily source of nourishment (Matt. 4:4).

As you go through this book, imagine we are getting together weekly at a coffee shop and teaching you how to study the Bible step by step in a very simple way. By the end of our time together, you will have the basic tools you need to study Scripture with the help of God's Spirit who lives within you.

Perhaps the greatest blessing my mom, sister, and I have seen with the EASY Bible Study Method is that anyone, no matter where they are in their faith journey, can learn how to study the Bible. We have heard stories of people who never thought they could study the Bible learn that through the help of the Holy Spirit, Scripture can be understood, grasped, applied, and something to delight in!

Friend, this can happen to you as you pick up God's Word and dive deep into it. Just like the psalmist, you will be able to declare, "I will delight in your statutes; I will not forget your word" (Ps. 119:16).

What to Expect

From Ashley, Taylor, and Mentor Mama Ellen

If you are wondering why we call it the EASY Bible Study Method, EASY is an acronym we use to help you remember each step to study, process, and apply Scripture to your life. Let's start by looking at what each letter stands for and what you'll learn through it.

EASY BIBLE STUDY METHOD

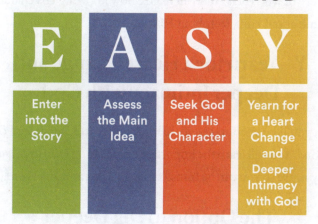

E—Enter into the Story

The first step is to *Enter into the Story*. You will learn how to step into a Bible story by reading the text slowly and thoughtfully. You will also discover the importance of context when reading Scripture and how to determine what the context is. In essence, you will become a good observer when reading the Bible and learn how to ask insightful questions.

A—Assess the Main Idea

Next, you will learn how to *Assess the Main Idea* of a Scripture passage by highlighting key points and themes through annotation, paraphrasing, and uncovering the passage's meaning. We know that may sound intimidating right now, but we promise you can do it! Stick with us! And as you work through those steps, the main idea will naturally emerge.

S—Seek God and His Character

Then, we will show you how to *Seek God and His Character* by looking for explicit and implicit qualities and characteristics of God. Seeking these out aims to allow you to grow closer to God the Father, Son, and Holy Spirit by understanding more of who He is. You will realize how knowing His character shapes how you think about Him, feel about Him, and act.

Y—Yearn for a Heart Change and Deeper Intimacy with God

Finally, you'll be encouraged to *Yearn for a Heart Change and Deeper Intimacy with God.* You will learn the importance of desiring Him to personally meet you where you are so you can be transformed by Him and His Word.[1]

The Option to Dig Deeper

DIG DEEPER We have organized the EASY Bible Study Method into two versions for you: the simple and the extended versions. You can choose which one will be a better fit for your specific

---

1. Coffee and Bible Time, "E.A.S.Y. Bible Study Method!," YouTube, October 25, 2024, https://www.youtube.com/watch?v=tN3mQG-MMGc.

What to Expect

needs. If you choose the extended version, it includes all of the Dig Deeper study prompts. Look for the Dig Deeper logo within each section of the EASY Bible Study Method.

How can you determine which version is for you? Here are some considerations to help you decide.

The EASY Bible Study Method: Is This for You?
- You are new to studying the Bible.
- You feel easily overwhelmed when studying Scripture.
- You feel easily confused when studying God's Word.
- You have a tight schedule.
- You want something simple.

The EASY Bible Study Method—Dig Deeper: Is This for You?
- You have studied the Bible in the past.
- You desire more of a challenge when studying Scripture.
- You want to dig deeper when studying God's Word.
- You have more time in your daily schedule.
- You are open to doing more reading and research.

We've included guides to each of these versions in the appendix. You can also scan this QR code for downloadable PDF versions.

Guide

Scan for a downloadable PDF of *The EASY Bible Study Method* guide or go to: coffeeandbibletime.com/easy-bible-study-guide/

Our Primary Scripture Focus

We will give you practical examples from the New Testament book of John as you learn how to use the EASY Bible Study Method. Our primary focus will be on John 6:1–15, where Jesus feeds the 5,000. Along with consistently studying John 6 throughout this book, we will also include other examples from Scripture passages throughout the Old and New Testaments. We do this because it is good for you to be exposed to all parts of Scripture.

This journey of learning how to study Scripture will have ripple effects on your life and others. You'll grow closer to our Savior, be amazed in awe and wonder at the infinite qualities of our great God, and be moved and motivated to share the great news of the gospel with others. We are so excited to be joining you on this journey!

CHAPTER ONE

Enter into the Story

From Ashley

Thirteen years old. That's the age I was when I picked my dusty Bible off the bookshelf and opened it to the first chapter of Genesis. Until that point in my life, I had been a Christian because of my family. They went to church on Sunday, so I went to church on Sunday. But that's about it. I didn't have a deep and abiding personal relationship with Christ yet.

I remember one week in Sunday school when my peers could answer questions about the Bible that I had no clue about. I felt lost and slightly embarrassed that I didn't know much of anything about the Bible. At that moment, my eyes were opened to the wonder of how vast and deep God's Word is. I longed to know what Scripture had to say and immerse myself in it as the other kids in my class seemed to be doing. That day, God started stirring within my heart a desire to know Him through His Word.

I went home determined to start reading the Bible. I created a plan to make it through the whole Bible. I would wake up at the crack of dawn before school and study one chapter a day. Along with reading, I would write a small summary of what I read every day in my spiral notebook.

Even though I wasn't a Bible scholar and didn't know about context or interpretation, I consistently showed up. I read Scripture, and I observed. I entered into the story, put myself in the shoes of the people I read about, and asked questions.

No matter how much biblical knowledge you might or might not have, you can do the same. You can enter into a story too. We all love stories. Most of us had narratives read to us as children. We love hearing funny accounts from our friends and family. We are captivated by movies and TV shows because of their strong and fascinating storylines.

The Bible is a story. It is one **divine and united story** of salvation through Jesus Christ, but it is also **made up of many smaller stories** that all fit into and add to the larger story. These stories are not fictional, nor are they just meant for our entertainment. Scripture encapsulates actual historical events and people. It is God's story for humanity, and it is God's story for you and me.

As a thirteen-year-old girl, I entered into Genesis. I could feel the boom of God's voice as He spoke creation into existence. I could hear the gentle sobs of Hagar alone in the wilderness. I could imagine the veins popping out of Abraham's head as he reluctantly trudged his only son up the mountain to be sacrificed. I discovered that the Bible's stories are full of action, tension, suspense, love, war, and heartbreak. There are epic battles between good and evil, and (spoiler alert) the end of the story is tremendously satisfying, as good ultimately prevails.

Most importantly, the Bible is a story that invited me into it. It answered life's biggest questions like "Who am I?" and "What am I here for?" It does the same for you. So, pick up your Bible, and let's enter into this grand story together.

E—Enter into the Story

What You Will Learn

The first step of the EASY Bible Study Method is *Enter into the Story*. In this chapter, you will learn how to do four things.

1 How to enter into a Bible story by reading the text slowly and thoughtfully

2 Why context is important in Bible study and how to determine what the context is

3 How to put yourself in the story

4 How to ask good questions

Before Diving In

But before diving into how to study a particular story in the Bible, it is essential to know the story of Scripture as a whole. The biblical story can be divided into four main parts: creation, fall, redemption, and new creation.

The Bible has 4 main turning points:
creation, fall, redemption, and new creation

Creation

"In the beginning, God created the heavens and the earth" (Gen. 1:1). The grand story of the Bible starts with God Himself. He created the earth and the first two human beings, Adam and Eve, to live in paradise with Him. Humans lived in a faultless world, and their relationship with God was perfect. It was how things were supposed to be.

Fall

God gave Adam and Eve the option to choose to trust in His goodness by obeying Him or to turn away from Him in disobedience. After the serpent tempted them, they chose disobedience and ate from the one tree in the garden that God forbade. From that moment on, death entered the world as a consequence of sin. Romans 5:12 says, "Therefore, just as sin came into the world through one man, and death through sin, and so death spread to all men because all sinned."

Humans were created to be in communion and intimate relationship with God. After the fall, humanity not only experienced the physical consequences of death but also the spiritual consequences of death, such as being separated from a holy and perfect God.

Although humanity turned against God, God did not give up on us. He always had a plan to redeem His people. As the rest of the Bible unfolds, you will read about God's steps to redeem His people.

Redemption

As soon as Adam and Eve sinned, God's plan to redeem His people and restore them to a right relationship with Him was initiated. He chose a people for Himself by calling a man named Abram (later known as Abraham). God promised that through Abraham, all the families of the earth would be blessed (Gen. 12:3). God grew Abraham's descendants into the Israelite nation and called them to be His chosen people. Although God had called Israel into a special relationship with Himself, they still failed to follow Him wholeheartedly.

Eventually, God sent His only Son, Jesus Christ, through Abraham's lineage to save both the Israelites and all who believe in Him as Lord and Savior. Through Jesus Christ, we can enter into a right relationship with God the Father. He redeemed us so that we may have eternal life with Himself. Jesus said, "And this is eternal life, that they know you, the only true God, and Jesus Christ whom you have sent" (John 17:3).

New Creation

Although Christ came and redeemed us, we still await the day He will return and make all things right and completely new. Sin still invades our lives, and so does the power of Satan, who has exerted his influence throughout all of humanity's history after the fall. Second Corinthians 4:4 says, "Satan, who is the god of this world, has blinded the minds of those who don't believe. They are unable to see the glorious light of the Good News. They don't understand this message about the glory of Christ, who is the exact likeness of God" (NLT).

Although Satan has temporary authority over this world now, Christ will ultimately judge and defeat Satan and all evil. He will reverse the curse of Adam. He will redeem the earth and all those who put their hope in Him. Ultimately, our relationship with God will be perfectly restored, and we will dwell with Him forever.

The grand story of the Bible is one you do not want to miss, and knowing its overall storyline is the first step in becoming serious about Bible study. Understanding it will help you better comprehend and find the meaning of each passage you read so that you can apply it to your life and know God's heart.

Let's begin to learn how to study this grand story and all the minor stories that play a role within the larger narrative. We'll start with learning how to read the text slowly and thoughtfully.

THE EASY BIBLE STUDY METHOD

Read the text slowly
and thoughtfully

The first thing we need to do when opening our Bibles and entering in is to slow down. Let me say that again ... s l o w d o w n.

The biggest foe of our Bible study time is our fast-paced culture and the craziness of life that comes with it. We must intentionally make room for reading Scripture by scheduling it on our calendar. Make a plan by picking a time in your day to go to your room, the library, or any quiet space to study. It could mean waking up half an hour earlier or getting off your phone thirty minutes before bed. Slow down. Take a deep breath. Quiet your heart and mind by saying a prayer.

Your prayer can be as simple as Psalm 119:18. It says:

Open my eyes, that I may behold
    wondrous things out of your law.

Sometimes, I pray, "Lord, open my eyes to Your Word. Help me slow down. Help me to become more like You as we study Your Word today." Part of slowing down is humbling our hearts and asking God for help.

Along with slowing down our lifestyle and making time to study, we also need to slow down our reading speed as we get into the text. Have you ever skimmed a book mindlessly? If so, you may have retained 5 percent of the book. Skimming is the opposite

> **Mentor Mama Ellen Note**
>
> *Pray and ask God to move in your heart, give you a thirst to know Him more, and help you to free space in your schedule to make Him a priority. Also, be kind to yourself and realistic that during different seasons in your life, you will have more time than others, and that's okay. What God cares about is your heart's desire to seek Him above all else.*

of what we need to do when we read the Bible. It's essential to slow down and thoughtfully take in every word.

There are a few ways you can read a text slowly and thoughtfully.

Read It Out Loud

Reading Scripture out loud will help you stay focused on what's written. Read slowly and think about every word.

Listen to the Text

Listen to the Bible with your eyes closed and your attention focused solely on the audio. You may be surprised to learn that Scripture's original audience did not read the Bible text themselves. Instead, they listened to Scripture being read to them. It wasn't until after the printing press and Martin Luther's reform that most individuals had personal access to the Word and studied it for themselves. Christians had been listening to the Bible for hundreds of years before reading it for themselves. Therefore, it is good for us not only to read the Word but also to hear it being read to us over and over again.

If you find that your mind wanders while listening to the text, we encourage you to **read and listen** at the same time. This will help your mind stay focused while listening to the audio.

Resources

Scan for a downloadable PDF of *The EASY Bible Study Method* resource links or go to: coffeeandbibletime.com/easy-bible-study-method-links/

You can find audio readings of Scripture online or on smartphone apps. For our recommendations, scan the QR code included here.

What Translation to Read

There are so many Bible translations available that it can feel overwhelming to choose one. If you are new to studying the Bible, we suggest selecting the New Living Translation (NLT) or the New International Version (NIV). These translations are simple to understand because they reflect our modern-day language.

If you are looking for a word-for-word translation (meaning it is the closest translation to the Bible's original text), I use the English Standard Version (ESV). I use this version when I am studying the biblical text in depth.

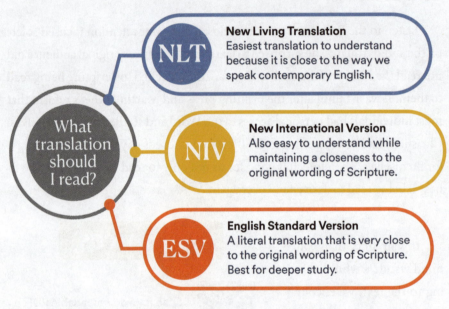

DIG DEEPER If you have the time and want to dig deeper into the text, here are two more ways to read Scripture slowly and thoughtfully.

Read the Text Multiple Times in Different Versions

If you want to take your Bible study further, we suggest reading the text in multiple translations. Sometimes, you can read a passage and not fully understand it if you only read one version. It is good to read different translations to give us a fuller idea of what the text is saying.

We talked about translations and recommended you choose NLT, NIV, or ESV. You could pick two of the translations we mentioned to read, or other excellent translations are the New King James Version (NKJV), New Century Version (NCV), Christian Standard Bible (CSB), New American Standard Bible (NASB), and *The Message* (MSG). You can find different versions of the Bible for free in apps and online. Check out our online list of resources for Bible apps and websites we recommend.

Get Interested in the Subject

Sometimes, it is hard to read a text because you may not be interested in the subject of what you are reading, such as genealogies or laws. Take some steps to get interested in the text by researching the history of the passage or listening to an online sermon or video teaching about the text you are reading. Knowing some background information can be highly beneficial in helping you enter into a text. Our resource list includes recommendations to help you dig deeper into different subjects.

TAKE ACTION Read John 6:1–15 about Jesus feeding the 5,000. This passage is included in the back of this book. Follow these steps:

1. Quiet your heart and say a prayer to start your Bible study time.

2. Read the text once out loud.

3. Listen to the text once with your eyes closed.

4. Listen to the text and read it at the same time.

5. Dig Deeper: Read the passage in different translations.

THE EASY BIBLE STUDY METHOD

Write down your observations here:

2

Determine the context

When diving into a passage, it is crucial to understand the context of what you are reading. What is *context*? Context includes the background information of the text you are reading. Knowing the context can shed more light on the passage.

As you study Scripture, you must remember that a **specific author** wrote each book of the Bible to **a particular group of people** who were **going through unique situations** at a specific time in history. As you read the Bible, it is necessary *first* to remember the original purpose of the text rather than immediately thinking about yourself and how the passage applies to you. Application is the last step of the Bible study process. First, you need to build a foundation of observation and understanding.

How to Determine the Context

When determining the context of a text, you can ask yourself a few questions, such as who the author is and who the original audience is. These questions help you learn about the background and history of the passage you read. You can answer these questions sometimes within the Bible itself, but other times, you will need to get outside sources to help you answer them. For example, a handful of psalms say David wrote them (like Psalm 3). But then there are books such as Hebrews that we do not know who the author is.

Study Bible

What's a Study Bible?

A Bible that includes additional background information such as context, themes, maps, and commentary to help the reader better understand the text.

I highly suggest you invest in a study Bible that includes additional background information, such as context, themes, maps, and commentary, to help you better understand the text. A study Bible has all the information you need about the context for each book of the Bible, such as the author, audience, setting, date, summary, history, and more. Some good study Bibles are the *NIV Application Study Bible*, the *NLT Life Application Study Bible*, and the *ESV Study Bible*.

Commentary

What's a Commentary?

A scholar's (or multiple scholars') explanation and interpretation of the biblical text including historical, cultural, and theological background to help the reader better understand the text.

Another great tool, similar to a study Bible, is a commentary. A commentary is a scholar's (or multiple scholars') explanation and interpretation of the biblical text, including historical, cultural, and theological background, to help the reader better understand the text.

You can always research these context questions online for free if you do not have a physical study Bible or commentary. If you choose to research online, make sure the sources you use are credible by looking to see who the article's author is and their credentials. Are they a reliable Christian scholar? What do they believe? Also, see what website it is and make sure it is a credible Christian ministry. Check out our online resource list for a free online commentary we love and some websites and videos we recommend for looking up context.

Context Questions to Ask

Here are a few context questions you can ask yourself when entering into a passage.

Where does this fit in the overall storyline of the Bible?
Remember earlier when we talked about the four main sections of the Bible: creation, fall, redemption, and new creation? It's important to keep these in mind when studying the Bible. The Bible covers over 1,500 years from beginning to end. It is a huge story, and it can get confusing when you read different parts of the Bible yet do not know where in the story you are.

Imagine you pick up a book series such as The Chronicles of Narnia and start reading the final book, *The Last Battle*. Although I can pick up *The Last Battle* and read it by itself, it would not have the same impact as reading it along with all the other books in the series. Why? Because I would miss out on the development of characters such as Aslan. I would be confused when the book references past events and themes from the earlier books. I also would not have a strong connection with the story or characters because I read it isolated from the larger story.

The same is true when reading the Bible. If you do not know the storyline,

OLD TESTAMENT

GENESIS – MALACHI

E—Enter into the Story

you will be confused. You will not know what past events are being referenced. You may feel lost when certain stories and characters are mentioned. Also, you will not have a strong connection to the story when you do not know the background information of what is going on and why.

I want to encourage you with this: The more you read your Bible, the better you will understand where each individual story fits in the overall story. After years of reading Scripture, I have memorized where each book of the Bible is in the overall story of God's Word. This knowledge happens naturally over time when you commit yourself to studying Scripture. And to be honest, I still need context help, so I will look up the context of whatever book I am currently reading.

You can ask yourself a few good questions to help you pinpoint where the passage you are reading falls on the biblical timeline:

Is this passage in the Old or New Testament?

- The books Genesis through Malachi are in the Old Testament, making up about 77 percent of the Bible. Matthew through Revelation are in the New Testament, about 23 percent of the Bible.

- You can find whether your passage is in the Old or New Testament by looking through the list of Old Testament and New Testament books.

NEW TESTAMENT

MATTHEW – REVELATION

31

THE EASY BIBLE STUDY METHOD

Old Testament

The Law (Torah or Pentateuch)
Genesis

Exodus

Leviticus

Numbers

Deuteronomy

The Historical Books
Joshua

Judges

Ruth

1 Samuel

2 Samuel

1 Kings

2 Kings

1 Chronicles

2 Chronicles

Ezra

Nehemiah

Esther

The Major Prophets
Isaiah

Jeremiah

Lamentations

Ezekiel

Daniel

The Minor Prophets
Hosea

Joel

Amos

Obadiah

Jonah

Micah

Nahum

Habakkuk

Zephaniah

Haggai

Zechariah

Malachi

The Poetic and Wisdom Books
Job

Psalms

Proverbs

Ecclesiastes

Song of Solomon (Song of Songs)

E—Enter into the Story

New Testament

The Gospels

Matthew

Mark

Luke

John

History

Acts

Pauline Epistles (Letters of Paul)

Romans

1 Corinthians

2 Corinthians

Galatians

Ephesians

Philippians

Colossians

1 Thessalonians

2 Thessalonians

1 Timothy

2 Timothy

Titus

Philemon

General Epistles (Letters)

Hebrews

James

1 Peter

2 Peter

1 John

2 John

3 John

Jude

Apocalyptic Literature

Revelation

Is this passage before Jesus took on human flesh or after?

- **Before Jesus was born**: *The Old Testament* was all written before Jesus took on human flesh. It points forward to Jesus coming as the long-awaited Jewish Messiah.
- **During Jesus' earthly life:** *The Gospels* (Matthew, Mark, Luke, and John) in the New Testament describe Jesus' life here on earth: His birth, life, ministry, death, resurrection, and ascension.
- **After Jesus ascended into heaven:** *The rest of the New Testament* (Acts–Revelation) is after Jesus ascended into heaven.
- **When Jesus will come back:** *Revelation*, the last book of the Bible, describes Jesus' future return.

Does this passage take place during creation, fall, redemption, or new creation?

- **Creation:** *Genesis 1–2* describes God's creation of the world and people.
- **Fall:** *Genesis 3* describes the fall of Adam and Eve and sin entering into the world. The rest of the Old Testament shows the consequences of sin on all humanity. The need for a Savior is clear throughout the entire Old Testament. God calls the Israelites to be His chosen people and promises a Savior to one day conquer sin.
- **Redemption:** *Matthew, Mark, Luke, and John* share how Jesus came into the world fully God and fully man, lived a perfect life, died the death we deserved, conquered death, rose from the grave, and ascended into heaven. The rest of the New Testament goes through the start of the church and the spreading of the gospel to the ends of the earth.
- **New Creation:** *Revelation* describes Jesus' return to earth and conquering of Satan, sin, and death forever. All believers will be living in a new heaven and a new earth in perfect unity with God and each other.

E—Enter into the Story

TAKE ACTION Where does John 6 fit in the overall storyline of the Bible? Is it a passage in the Old or New Testament? Does it happen before Jesus took on human flesh, during His earthly life, or after He ascended into heaven? Does the passage take place in creation, fall, redemption, or new creation?

Write down your answers here:

_____
_____
_____
_____
_____

Ashley's Insights

John 6 is a passage in the New Testament. It occurs during Jesus' earthly life, during the Bible's redemption period.

Who was the original author? What do you know about the author?

The Bible was written by approximately

40 different authors over **1,500** years

Approximately forty different authors wrote the Bible over 1,500 years. Many of the books have a specific author and some have multiple authors. Learning

The Easy Bible Study Method

about the original author also sheds light on the text. Certain books of the Bible will directly tell who the author is, such as Romans or Ephesians, which Paul wrote. Other times, it is not so clear and will require outside sources to help you understand who wrote it, such as Genesis or Deuteronomy. Together, we will look into the book of John and answer these context questions about authorship.

TAKE ACTION Who wrote the book of John? Look up who the author of the gospel of John is either online, in a commentary, or using a study Bible. What did you learn about the author?

_____

_____

_____

_____

Ashley's Insights

The gospel of John was written by John, the disciple whom Jesus loved.

In the book of John, you will notice that the author does not mention who he is. The author calls himself "the disciple Jesus loved" (John 21:7) multiple times. It is clear that the author was one of Jesus' twelve disciples, but which one? Here is where you can turn to outside resources for help. Most sources will tell you that church history and many credible scholars agree that John wrote the gospel of John.

John was one of Jesus' closest disciples. He walked with Jesus through His entire ministry. He was there when Jesus died on the cross, rose again, and ascended into heaven. It is absolutely incredible that we have a firsthand witness to the life of Jesus Christ through His beloved disciple, John.

However, you cannot assume that the name of each book of the Bible is also

E—Enter into the Story

the name of the author. In this case with John, it is true that John is the author. But this is not always the case. For example, the book of Acts is written by a man named Luke.

Who was the original audience, and what were they going through?

The Bible was not first written to you. Each book of the Bible was written to a particular group of people at a particular time. Knowing this helps you learn the purpose of the text. Sometimes, a book of the Bible will clearly say who the author is writing to, but other times it may not be so straightforward and will require further research.

TAKE ACTION Who was John's audience? Look up the answer online, in a commentary, or in a study Bible.

Ashley's Insights

John is writing to Jews and Gentiles (*Gentile* means a non-Jew), encouraging them to believe in Jesus as the Messiah and Son of God.

John is writing to Jews because he builds on many Old Testament themes, for example:

- Jewish festivals such as the Passover (John 2:13) and the Feast of Tabernacles (John 7:2 NIV)

- Jewish concepts such as the Lamb of God (John 1:29)
- References to the Jewish Scriptures (John 1:45)

We know he is writing to Gentiles because:

- John sometimes describes Jewish customs and terms to non-Jewish readers (John 1:38, 1:41, 4:9)

DIG DEEPER When was this written? What major events were going on during this time? Knowing the period of a passage will give you more understanding into the historical and cultural background, therefore helping you understand the text better. Ask yourself: *What time period in history was this passage from? What other events were happening during this time?* Using a study Bible, commentary, or online research will be essential for this step.

TAKE ACTION When did John write this gospel? What did you find out about the date of authorship and the period when John was written?

Ashley's Insights
- John wrote this near the end of his life, looking back on his time with Jesus
- Around AD 70 to AD 100
- Jerusalem had been attacked by the Romans, and the temple had been destroyed

E—Enter into the Story

| **DIG DEEPER** | Are there any historical or cultural customs, locations, or elements within the text that could be researched more to understand the meaning?

Many topics within each book of the Bible can be further studied to understand the text better. Remember, the Bible was written thousands of years ago. Customs and culture, or the ways people lived, look very different from our lives today. Studying these key elements will assist you in understanding the text better.

In the book of John, there are people, Old Testament references, cultural customs, and locations that we don't fully understand today as modern readers, such as:

- Jerusalem, Galilee, Capernaum, Samaria
- Elijah, Moses, Isaiah
- Passover
- Temple
- Pharisees
- Rabbi and disciples
- Samaritans, Romans, Greeks
- The Law
- Light, bread, blood, wine
- Shepherds
- Death

Let's take, for example, the word *Pharisee* and look deeper into what this word means. In John 3, we are introduced to a man named Nicodemus. The text says that he was a Pharisee. Do you know what this term means or what a Pharisee did in Israelite culture? We can do a few things to help us learn what this word means.

Look to see where else this word shows up in Scripture. I like to look online for Scripture passages that mention the same word throughout the Bible. You can reference our resource list to see website recommendations for cross-referencing. I looked through multiple Scripture passages that mention the word Pharisee. Here is what I learned:

39

1. Matthew 23:1–7 says they do their deeds to be seen by others. They preach and do not practice.

2. Luke 18:10–14 tells me they are prideful and have a false sense of righteousness. They do not know their need for God.

3. Luke 20:46–47 says they look righteous on the outside, but on the inside, their hearts are far from God.[2]

Spend time doing online research. When I research this topic online what do I learn? Check out our online resource list for credible website recommendations. I searched "Who were the Pharisees?" and found an article full of helpful information:

1. I learned, "The Pharisees were an influential religious sect within Judaism in the time of Christ and the early church. They were known for their emphasis on personal piety (the word *Pharisee* comes from a Hebrew word meaning 'separated'), their acceptance of oral tradition in addition to the written Law, and their teaching that all Jews should observe all 600-plus laws in the Torah, including the rituals concerning ceremonial purification."[3]

2. The Pharisees knew a lot about God and the Law, but their knowledge of God was far from their hearts.

Bible Dictionary

What's a Bible Dictionary?

A book that includes the definitions and original biblical meanings to words, concepts, and themes within the Bible such as people, places, events, locations, items, and more.

Look the word up in a Bible dictionary. Bible dictionaries define significant major terms, definitions, customs, people, locations, items, and concepts from the Bible. I find them extremely helpful because if I am confused about a word or

---

2. D. A. Carson, *The Gospel According to John*, The Pillar New Testament Commentary (W.B. Eerdmans, 1991).

3. "Who Were the Pharisees?," Got Questions Ministries, accessed November 15, 2024, https://www.gotquestions.org/Pharisees.html.

E—Enter into the Story

concept, I can easily look it up in the dictionary. For more suggestions, check out our online recommended resource list. As a reminder, we included a QR code to it earlier in this chapter.

TAKE ACTION Are there any historical or cultural things, customs, locations, or elements within John 6:1–15 that could be researched more in order to understand the meaning?

Ashley's Insights

After doing further digging, I found a few terms that I looked into and researched:

- **Sea of Galilee** (John 6:1): A small freshwater lake that was a central place for fishing and trade. The Sea of Galilee is where Jesus called Peter, Andrew, James, and John and where major events in the Gospels happened, such as Jesus feeding the 5,000 and Jesus walking on water. See the map in the Appendix.

- **The Signs** (John 6:2, 14): Jesus' public ministry (John 2–12) is called "The Book of Signs," which reveals Jesus' glory.[4] These signs were miracles that Jesus had done, and they proved His authority. They brought about faith and belief in His disciples and people, but some people were so focused on the signs that they missed Jesus (John 4:48).

---

4. D. A. Carson, *The Gospel According to John*, The Pillar New Testament Commentary (Wm. B. Eerdmans, 1991).

THE EASY BIBLE STUDY METHOD

- **The Passover** (John 6:4): The Passover is a Jewish feast that celebrates and reflects on God's deliverance of the Israelite people from slavery in Egypt. The Israelites were commanded to celebrate Passover every year by returning to Jerusalem and having a feast that reflected on the Passover's events. Directly following this was the Feast of Unleavened Bread. The Israelites were to eat bread without yeast for seven days, symbolizing Israel's exit from Egypt, the purging of sin, and return to holiness.

- **Denarii** (John 6:7): A day's wage.

- **The Prophet who is to come into the world** (John 6:14): The Israelites were waiting for a prophet to come and save them (especially from their oppression under the Romans). There are many Old Testament passages that gave the Israelites hope that a prophet would come and one day save them. For example, Moses testifies about Jesus in Deuteronomy 18:15–18.

DIG DEEPER What is the surrounding context of the verse or passage you are studying? You can find this context by reading the verses or chapters that come before and after it.

It is imperative to read Scripture within its context and not give it your own meaning. This will come naturally if you are reading and studying through entire books of the Bible at a time rather than jumping around Scripture and reading individual passages or chapters out of context. If you choose to jump around, make sure you familiarize yourself with the context of each verse or passage you are reading.

TAKE ACTION Read John 5 and John 6:16–71, which are the surrounding context of John 6:1–15. Summarize what you read and explain how this adds to your understanding of John 6:1–15.

E—Enter into the Story

Summarize John 5:

Summarize John 6:16–71:

How do these passages add to John 6:1–15?

Ashley's Insights

John 5 Summary

Jesus healed a man on the Sabbath, which upset the Pharisees. They especially didn't like that Jesus called God His Father, making Himself equal with God (John 5:18). Jesus shared more about His unique relationship with the Father and the authority that Jesus has through the Father. Jesus then goes on to describe the three main witnesses that testify about Him: John the Baptist, Jesus' miracles, and Scripture. Last, Jesus mentions Moses—how if they believed in Moses, they would believe in Jesus because Moses wrote about Jesus.

John 6:16–71 Summary

Jesus' disciples were caught in a storm on the Sea of Galilee that night, and Jesus came to them walking on the water. At first, they were frightened, but when they realized it was Jesus, they let Him into the boat. The next day, the crowds from the feeding found Jesus. Jesus declared Himself to be **the true Bread of Life** that came from heaven **just like the manna came down from heaven in the wilderness with Moses and the Israelites**. Jesus said they could receive eternal life through His body and blood, which offended them. Many left Jesus. However, **His closest disciples continued to believe in Jesus as the Holy One sent from God**.

How do these passages add to John 6:1–15?

From reading both John 5 and the rest of John 6, many things become clearer:

1. Jesus not only miraculously provided bread to thousands of people, but He is THE Bread of Life. Spiritually speaking, Jesus is the only one who can satisfy the human soul. His body and blood, which He gave for us on the cross, saves us. Jesus performed this miracle not just to feed the people physically but to point to something so much greater—that He is the Bread of Life!

2. Many of God's people continue to reject Him. Not only did the Pharisees lack belief in Jesus, but so did many of Jesus' followers after hearing Jesus' hard teachings.

3. Jesus continues to challenge, test, and teach His closest disciples. They truly do believe in Jesus despite His hard teachings and lack of popularity among the Jews.

4. There are many strong **connections to the Old Testament**.

    a. Deuteronomy 18:15–18: Moses had predicted that a Prophet would one day come. In Deuteronomy 18:15, he says, "The

LORD your God will raise up for you a prophet like me from among your fellow Israelites. You must listen to him" (NLT). The people struggled to believe in Jesus as this Prophet, and they ultimately did not believe in the Jesus that Moses had written about hundreds of years prior.

b. **Exodus 16:** Jesus compares Himself to the manna in the wilderness that came down from heaven, recorded in Exodus 16. Jesus shared how He is the greater "bread from heaven" (John 6:32 NLT) coming to satisfy their spiritual needs.

c. **Leviticus 23:** Jesus declared Himself to be the "bread of life" (John 6:35 NLT) around the time of the Passover and Feast of Unleavened Bread. The Israelites were to cease eating leaven (yeast) in their bread as a remembrance of their escape from slavery in Egypt and as a symbol of fleeing from sin (yeast represents sin). Jesus declares Himself to be the Bread of Life during this major Israelite festival—and He truly is the pure, unleavened, sinless bread of life.

I want to share another example from John 21:15–19 that highlights the importance of the surrounding context. In this passage, Jesus asks Peter three times in a row if Peter truly does love Him. It is already a strong question for Jesus to ask Peter so boldly, yet Jesus not only says it once—but *three times.* If this is all I know, I can still get the point that Jesus really wants to see if Peter is dedicated, but understanding the surrounding context of this passage makes it much richer.

So, what is the surrounding context?

First, the book of John has twenty-one chapters, so we are at the end of the gospel of John. Jesus has already died and been resurrected. He will soon leave the earth. These are some of His last words to Peter.

Second, if I am familiar with the book of John or the Gospels, I will know that Peter is one of Jesus' beloved disciples. He is a part of Jesus' inner circle. Jesus had even declared to Peter that he would be the rock of the church (Matt. 16:18).

Third, just a few chapters earlier (John 18), when Jesus was arrested and about to be condemned to death on the cross, Peter denied knowing Jesus *three times* in a row. Three times! When Jesus needed His close friend the most, Peter left and claimed never to have walked with Jesus.

So now as I read John 21:15–19 with the surrounding context in mind, I see that it was no coincidence that Jesus asked Peter if he loved Him *three times*. Jesus already knew Peter's heart. It was Jesus' intention to test his heart at that moment because soon Peter would have to literally take up his cross for the sake of Jesus Christ.

Genres of the Bible

From Mentor Mama Ellen

Being familiar with the multiple types of literary genres helps us understand what to expect from a specific text within that genre. The Bible genres include the law, historical narratives, prophetic teaching, poetry, wisdom literature, gospels, epistles or letters, and apocalyptic literature. And it is not uncommon for books of the Bible to contain multiple genres.

One approach you can take when studying Scripture is to focus on the literary genre of the book you are reading. The writers, no matter whether they were historians, poets, wisdom teachers, or prophets, were concerned not only about what they said but also about how they went about saying it. You can read the Bible from a literary perspective by concentrating on what the text can teach us about the text.

Reading a text literarily helps us feel like we are witnesses to a story, watching each act as it unfolds. We read with an approach that questions the text to determine the genre, human experiences, patterns of the text, artistry, and any clues that can guide our understanding of what Scripture is saying. Let's look at each of these genres now in greater detail.

Genres of the Bible

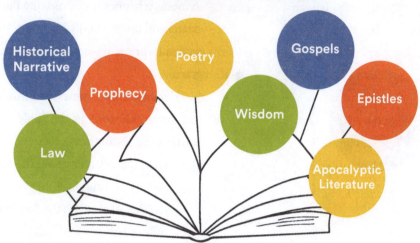

Law

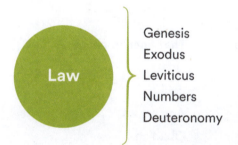

The first five books of the Bible, also known as the Pentateuch, are referred to as the Law. These books of laws and rules, written by Moses, were given to God's people after their exodus from slavery so that they understood how to live distinctly different from the surrounding pagan nations. In the Law, God provided standards for holy living, which required people to obey and fear Him. Ultimately, sinful man could not meet these perfect requirements. Only blood sacrifices to atone for their sin could restore fellowship with God.

Historical Narrative

The narrative of many of the books in the Bible is storylike, with cause-and-effect elements that are related to each other through the use of plot, characters, setting, and narrator. Much of the Old Testament, Joshua through Esther, along with parts of the Pentateuch, is historical, recounting events from creation to Israel's return from

The Easy Bible Study Method

Historical Narrative
- Joshua
- Judges
- Ruth
- 1 Samuel
- 2 Samuel
- 1 Kings
- 2 Kings
- 1 Chronicles
- 2 Chronicles
- Ezra
- Nehemiah
- Esther

exile. Unlike the worldview portrayed in modern history textbooks, the Bible clearly and unashamedly highlights the past as a witness of God's judgment and grace.

Here are a few examples of historical narrative books in the Bible and stories included in them:

- Genesis: Abraham, Sarah, and Isaac; Jacob and Joseph
- Exodus: Moses and the Israelites
- Judges: Samson and Delilah
- 1 Samuel: David and Goliath

Prophecy

Prophecy

The Major Prophets	The Minor Prophets
Isaiah	Hosea
Jeremiah	Joel
Lamentations	Amos
Ezekiel	Obadiah
Daniel	Jonah
	Micah
	Nahum
	Habakkuk
	Zephaniah
	Haggai
	Zechariah
	Malachi

The prophetic writings in the Bible not only include predictions about future events that God gave the prophets in visions and dreams but also include

48

warnings of upcoming judgment and an overview of God's plan for Israel. The messages of the prophets were also rooted in the present as they wanted to appeal to the hearts of their listeners to take action, usually to repent and turn back to God.

Poetry

In general, poetry is more challenging for most people to understand. It may be surprising that the Bible contains many such works, considering the gravity of the message the authors were trying to communicate. Poetry is also very effective in arousing emotions and moving the will of its readers. There are three primary traits of biblical poetry: terseness, parallelism, and imagery and figurative language.

Terseness is seen in the lines of Hebrew poetry that are short or terse but pack a big punch. For example, Psalm 23:1 says, "The Lord is my shepherd." The conciseness of this phrase does not negate its impact. Being "my shepherd" recognizes God as my guide, protector, and caregiver who knows me by name.

Parallelism is the use of two lines or sentences in poetry that link to each other in some way. These lines have long been observed as the telltale sign of Hebrew poetry. The two main types of parallelism are synonymous and antithetic. *Synonymous* is when the same thought is repeated in two or more lines and may even build or intensify upon the first line. Isaiah 1:16–17 is an example of this:

Wash yourselves; make yourselves clean;
    remove the evil of your deeds from before my eyes;
cease to do evil,
    learn to do good;
seek justice,

correct oppression;
bring justice to the fatherless,
plead the widow's cause.

Antithetic parallelism contrasts opposing ideas to draw attention to their obvious differences. In Proverbs 10:1, we see "wise son" verses "foolish son":

A wise son makes a glad father,
but a foolish son is a sorrow to his mother.

Poetry uses *imagery and figurative language* to increase a passage's emotional effect. These tools form visual images in one's mind of what the writer is trying to communicate. Some examples of these are:

- **Simile:** A comparison between two things marked with "like" or "as." We see a simile in Matthew 13:44, which says, "The kingdom of heaven is like treasure hidden in a field."
- **Metaphor:** An image is used to explain something, but is not to be taken literally. For example, John 6:35 says, "Jesus said to them, 'I am the bread of life.'"
- **Symbolism:** A concrete image that represents abstract concepts and ideas. An example of this is 2 Samuel 22:3: ". . . my God, my rock, in whom I take refuge."
- **Hyperbole:** An exaggeration for the sake of effect. We read an example of hyperbole in Matthew 7:3, where Jesus asks, "Why do you see the speck that is in your brother's eye, but do not notice the log that is in your own eye?"
- **Personification:** Attributing personality to inanimate objects. An example of this is Isaiah 55:12:

The mountains and the hills before you
shall break forth into singing,
and all the trees of the field shall clap their hands.

50

Wisdom

Wisdom literature provides guidance for daily living according to the rules established by God. It gives insights into topics such as meditation on creation, human relationships, and how to live life and effectively deal with its challenges. No matter the type of specific wisdom each of these book authors was seeking, their overall objective was to increase their understanding and properly apply the wisdom learned. Proverbs 2:6–8 identifies the source of wisdom and what God provides to those who walk accordingly:

> For the LORD gives wisdom;
>> from his mouth come knowledge and understanding;
>
> he stores up sound wisdom for the upright;
>> he is a shield to those who walk in integrity,
>
> guarding the paths of justice
>> and watching over the way of his saints.

Gospels

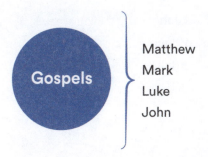

The Gospels in the New Testament are primarily narrative and generally follow a chronological pattern from Jesus' birth, public ministry, death, and resurrection. The four accounts of the Gospels are complementary stories that provide different perspectives and angles, such as how multiple cameras at the same sporting event highlight various aspects of the identical occasion.

The Gospels include setting, plot, and characters, with Jesus as the recognizable protagonist who teaches through what He says and does. It follows that the reactions of the people He encountered fell into two categories: those with growing faith and those with increasing hostility.

Dispersed in the narrative of the Gospels are the discourses, parables, and conversations of Jesus, where He imparts the truth of who He is, why He came, and how everyone can know the Father who sent Him. Our hero turns our expectations upside down with His unconventional actions as He forgives sins, heals the sick, makes demons flee, and raises people from the dead. Equally unexpected are His claims to be both human and divine, how He invites people into His spiritual kingdom, His substitutionary death on the cross, and His resurrection from death. This death was brought on by the hypocritical, formalized religious leaders of the time.

Epistles

Epistles

Pauline Epistles (Letters by Paul)
Romans
1 Corinthians
2 Corinthians
Galatians
Ephesians
Philippians
Colossians
1 Thessalonians
2 Thessalonians
1 Timothy
2 Timothy
Titus
Philemon

General Epistles (Letters by Other Apostles)
Hebrews
James
1 Peter
2 Peter
1 John
2 John
3 John
Jude

The epistles are letters written by either an apostle or one of Jesus' family members to churches or individuals during the New Testament times on theology, doctrine, and correction and training in righteousness. They were often dictated to a scribe, thus are oratorical in tone and style, and then reviewed by the author before being sent by a messenger. The letters generally followed a format of introduction, salutation, the main body that included thanksgiving and wisdom to address moral issues, and a concluding blessing with personal notes.

Apocalyptic

Isaiah (chapters 24–27)
Ezekiel (chapters 37–41)
Daniel (chapters 7–12)
Zechariah (chapters 9–12)
Revelation

Apocalyptic literature contains visions from God that reveal insight into the ending of evil times and the deliverance of God's future kingdom. It is poetic, using symbols, images, and numbers to describe future events. These were used when it was judicious to disguise the message and were not meant to confuse the reader. These beyond-life messages were given to believers to instruct and encourage them during difficult times. The word *apocalyptic* often refers to the end times and includes Christ's second coming and the battle of Armageddon.

TAKE ACTION Which of the seven literary genres we just learned about (historical, poetry, wisdom, epistles, gospel, prophecy, and apocalyptic) applies to John? Explain why.

Ellen's Insights

The literary genre of John is gospel. It is a narrative that follows Jesus' public ministry, death, and resurrection. John proclaims the good news of Jesus and how in Jesus there is eternal life for all who believe.

A Final Thought on Context

From Ashley

All this information in context can feel overwhelming. I totally understand. We simply want to give you the foundational knowledge of how to study the Bible, and this is the best place to start regarding context. Take heart, friend. Here are some ideas on how and when you can use what you've learned about context:

- If you are reading a book of the Bible, much of what we talked about can be done at the beginning when you are first getting to know the book (such as learning who the author is, the audience, genre, etc.). But then, as you continue studying the book, you won't have to do all this background study because you will already know it.

- Sometimes, you will encounter words and topics you do not know, which you can look up online or in a Bible dictionary.

- If you are busy or do not have the energy to look up all this information, you should at least identify the author and audience of the passage you are reading to have a little bit of background knowledge when reading the text.

E—Enter into the Story

Put yourself in the story

After reading the text slowly and studying the context, it is time to immerse yourself in the story. This step is not complicated; it just requires you to be imaginative and jump into the passage as if you were there.

First, ask yourself what five senses you experience in this story. What do you hear, taste, smell, see, and feel?

Imagine you are a person in the crowd within the story of John 6, where Jesus feeds the 5,000. You have been following Jesus because of the miracles He has been doing. You and thousands of others are drawn to Him like magnets. You need to find out who He is and why He is here. All you know is that He is unlike any other human you have ever met.

After walking for miles, you **feel** that your feet hurt and your stomach won't stop grumbling. You eavesdrop on Jesus and His disciples and **hear** them mention something about bread. You **see** a little boy full of hope offer up only five loaves of bread and two fish. Not long after this, Jesus walks up to you, looks you in the eyes, smiles, and hands you a loaf of bread and a fish. You **smell** the sweet aroma of freshly baked warm bread and taste the saltiness of the fresh fish. But the incredible thing is that you are not the only one who receives bread and fish; so do the 5,000 men who were with you (not to mention all the women and children too). After seeing this miracle happen, you and the others cannot stop talking about how Jesus "is indeed the Prophet who is to come into the world!" (John 6:14).

You can also ask yourself: *What would I feel or think in this situation?* **Put yourself in the shoes of the people you are reading about.**

In John 6, how would you feel if you were with the crowd and experienced Jesus feeding and providing for everyone?

If you were one of Jesus' disciples, what would you feel when you realized there was no food to feed the people? Would you be anxious? Would you have

THE EASY BIBLE STUDY METHOD

trusted Jesus to take care of the situation?

If you were Andrew in the passage, would you have had the courage and the hope to bring the little boy to Jesus, who only had a small amount of food? Would you be thinking that Jesus could do a miracle?

Give yourself the freedom to feel the situation's weight, wonder, joy, sorrow, pain, or happiness. What primary emotion stands out to you in the event of John 6? For me, it is a complete *wonder* that Christ actually fed over 10,000 people (enough to fill a modern-day stadium) with only five loaves and two fish. It must have been a jaw-dropping experience.

It is absolutely incredible that Christ did this. When you put yourself in the story, you are more likely to be amazed by this miracle, just as the original audience was!

Read through John 6:1–15 again. As you read, put yourself in the story and ask yourself these questions and journal your thoughts.

TAKE ACTION What five senses do you experience in this story? What do you hear, taste, smell, feel, and see?

What would you feel or think in this situation? Put yourself in the shoes of the disciples or the crowd.

E—Enter into the Story

Ask good questions

Last, entering the story is the time to ask good questions. No matter where you are on your journey as a Christian, there is never a moment when you will finally know it all. Even the most brilliant scholars ask questions and ponder Scripture.

Do not be afraid to write down questions as you read and ask them to a trusted mentor, pastor, or friend. You can research your questions in books and credible online sources. Every good learner asks good questions.

You will have many unique questions about what you are specifically learning and reading. But here are a few good questions you can also ask while reading a passage of Scripture:

- Why is the author writing this?
- What was the audience going through?
- What did this mean to them?
- Who is this person?
- Where is this location?
- What Old Testament theme is this referring to?
- What is the definition of this word? What does it mean?
- During what time did this happen?

These are just a few questions. Sometimes, the most common question is: *What in the world is going on?!* And that is entirely okay to ask. The Bible is filled with crazy and sometimes confusing stories that you probably never even would have guessed were in there. It is okay to ask questions and to search for the answers.

Keep in mind that sometimes you will ask questions, and you may not get the answers you want. There may even be times that you won't find an answer because some things in Scripture will always remain a mystery to us.

What does asking good questions while reading a Bible passage look like? Here's an example. Perhaps you are reading through the book of John, and you come across different names for Jesus, such as "the Word," "the Lamb of God," "the Son of God," "Son of Man," "King of Israel," "Messiah," "Rabbi," and "the Prophet."

You can ask yourself good questions such as: What do these names mean? Do they each have a different meaning? What is their importance? Do any of them have an Old Testament connection? What did they mean to the original audience?

So, you make a list and do some research. You discover:

> ### Mentor Mama Ellen Note
>
> *After thirty years of doing Bible studies, I can firmly attest that the group study environment is an awesome additional place for seeking answers to your most burning questions. And even further, I benefited from learning answers to questions I hadn't even thought to ask. Within groups, there's a solid Bible-teaching leader, and members usually have a range of biblical understanding. So, if your goal is to broaden your Scripture knowledge, consider joining a Bible study at your local church or through the Coffee and Bible Time Community.*

- **The Word:** It is connected to Genesis 1:1 and Greek philosophical thought. Jesus is the ultimate communication of God to humans.

- **The Lamb of God:** This is connected to Isaiah 53:7. Lambs were used for sacrifice in the Old Testament to take away sin. It is also connected to the Passover (Ex. 12:5–7). Jesus is our ultimate and final sacrifice, dying for our sins.

- **The Son of God:** God is made manifest in human form through Jesus, who is the exact nature of God. This is connected to Hebrews 1:3 and focuses on Jesus' deity in John 1.

- **Son of Man:** This title focuses on Jesus' humanity and shows that Jesus was fully human. This is connected to Daniel 7:13–14.

E—Enter into the Story

TAKE ACTION For the next four names of Jesus, do some research and answer the questions: *What do these terms mean and signify? What Old Testament connection do they have?*

King of Israel (John 1:49; 12:13–15):

Messiah (John 1:41; 4:25–26):

Rabbi (John 1:38; 1:49; 3:2):

Prophet (John 4:19; 6:14; 9:17):

Ashley's Insights

King of Israel (John 1:49; 12:13–15):
Jesus is the fulfillment of Old Testament prophecies where God promised a king through the line of David to rule forever (2 Sam. 7:12–16). The Jewish people wanted a political king to overthrow the Romans, but Jesus came as a spiritual king to save the world from sin and death.

Messiah (John 1:41; 4:25–26):
Messiah means "Anointed One" in Hebrew. Jesus is the Savior of the world, the Jewish Anointed One that the Israelites were waiting for (Isa. 53).

Rabbi (John 1:38; 1:49; 3:2):
Rabbi means teacher. Usually, rabbis taught the law and had students (disciples) who followed them closely.

> *Prophet (John 4:19; 6:14; 9:17):*
>
> Jesus fulfills Old Testament prophecies, where God promised a prophet greater than Moses (Deut. 18:15). Jesus proclaimed the Kingdom of God, and His message came directly from God the Father.

Conclusion

In this chapter, you learned how to enter into a Bible passage by reading the text slowly and thoughtfully, researching the context of the text, putting yourself in the story, and asking good questions. You should now be able to *enter into* any text you read confidently! You have the first steps to start studying the Bible! In the next chapter, we will learn how to *Assess the Main Idea* of a passage so we can begin to interpret the Bible properly!

E—Enter into the Story

Steps for E: Enter into the Story

At the end of each chapter, we will leave you with a simple list of the steps for each EASY Bible Study Method section. When studying the Bible, you can use this as a reference guide.

STEP ONE: E – ENTER INTO THE STORY

- **Pray** before reading
- **Read** the text slowly and thoughtfully
- **Determine** the context
  - Where does this fit in the storyline of the Bible?
  - Who was the original author?
  - Who was the original audience and what were they going through?
- **Put** yourself in the story
- **Ask** good questions

DIG DEEPER

- Read the text in different translations: ESV, NLT, NIV, NKJV
- When was this written? What was the date? What major events were going on during this time?
- Are there any historical or cultural things, customs, locations, or elements within the text that could be researched more in order to understand the meaning?
- What is the surrounding context of the verse or passage you are studying?
- What is the literary genre of this text and how does that add to the meaning of the passage?

Discussion Questions

To help you reflect on the chapter, here are optional discussion questions that you can discuss with a friend, mentor, or small group.

1. What stood out to you from chapter 1? Do you have any questions?

2. When did you first start reading or desiring to read the Bible?

3. What were your first impressions of the Bible? (It's okay to be honest.)

4. Explain why you now desire to know God more and study Scripture.

5. What challenges do you have with reading the Bible or studying Scripture?

6. Can you explain the four main parts of the Bible (and the gospel message)? Try now!

7. What have you learned so far from entering into the John 6:1–15 story? What did you feel, hear, see, taste, smell, and think when you put yourself in the story?

8. What questions did you have about John 6:1–15?

9. What is the context of John 6? Who wrote it? Who did he write it to?

CHAPTER TWO

Assess the Main Idea

From Ashley

Have you ever picked up a book, read a few pages, and thought, *What in the world did I just read?* I have! Reading has been a yearslong struggle for me. As a little girl, it did not come easily. In terms of my reading level, I was behind the other children in my class and needed extra help and attention from tutors and an additional summer in school.

Throughout middle school and high school, I struggled through English class. I didn't mind figuring out the value of X in algebra. Deep within the acts of *Romeo and Juliet*, though, I found myself completely lost—not to mention confused by the nitty-gritty demands of grammar and syntax! (What's an adverb again?)

Although reading didn't come naturally to me, I beat the odds. I can confidently say that I am now a strong reader and love reading! I learned to love it through four years of rigorous college training while getting my undergrad degree. For every class, I was assigned three to five textbooks. In total, I read well over 150 academic books during that time. There were many moments of frustration and toil. I didn't always understand what I was reading and constantly felt behind and overwhelmed. But I didn't give up!

These classes required me to read books outside my comfort zone and annotate on every page. I forced myself to push through the discomfort of not understanding. By summarizing different texts, making notes while reading, defining unknown words, and finding the main ideas of books, I learned how to read and understand what I was reading.

While learning these academic reading skills, I thought they would serve no purpose in my life. But now, I owe it to these professors and classes that I can study and understand the Bible. I discovered that reading is not only a skill we use in high school or college but a skill we will need for the rest of our lives as we study God's Word and get to know Him more and more. After all, what's the point of reading the Bible if we don't understand it?

As we've discussed, the Bible is a large book with many stories and themes. It can be confusing to understand sometimes and overwhelming to read. Because of this, studying and understanding the Bible takes hard work and discipline. It is unlike scrolling on social media, where information is passively absorbed. Bible study takes time, intentionality, and hard work! But I'm confident that if I could beat the odds and learn to understand ancient literature (such as the Bible), then so can you! By learning and implementing the tools we'll cover in this chapter, you can also become a confident reader of the Bible!

What You Will Learn

So far, in the EASY Bible Study Method, we have learned how to *E—Enter into the Story*. In this step, we observed the text to grasp what we are reading and "entering" into. The second step of the EASY Bible Study method is *A—Assess the Main Idea*. In this chapter, you will learn three steps.

A–Assess the Main Idea

1 How to paraphrase a Bible passage in your own words

2 How to annotate or identify key words and themes in a passage

3 How to discover the meaning of a passage

Before Diving In

After properly observing a Bible passage, the next best step is interpretation. *Interpretation* is just a fancy word for **finding the intended meaning of a passage so we can fully understand what's going on.**

Bible scholar D. A. Carson said this about interpretation: "We are dealing with God's thoughts: we are obligated to take the greatest pains to **understand** them truly and to explain them clearly."[5] Carson stresses the importance of understanding Scripture. Why? Because it is God's thoughts we are encountering. The Bible isn't just any other book. It is from the very heart of God, breathed out by His Spirit (2 Tim. 3:16–17). The Bible is a special gift we must take care of and steward well.

We can properly handle Scripture by studying the Bible *exegetically* (ek-suh-JET-ik-lee). If this word is new to you and feels daunting, biblical **exegesis** means to **draw out a text's meaning**. We can do this by first understanding the original meaning intended by the biblical authors to the original audience. We must remember that the Bible wasn't written directly *to* us but is 100 percent *for* us.

Why am I mentioning all this? Many people tend to pick and choose what they want from Scripture. They select a verse that stands out to them, drag it out of context, and make it mean whatever they want. This often renders the passage

---

5. D. A. Carson, *Exegetical Fallacies*, 2nd ed. (Baker Academic, 1996), 15. Emphasis added.

completely different in meaning than the original biblical author intended.

For example, the Bible verse Jeremiah 29:11 is very popular. It says, "For I know the plans I have for you, declares the LORD, plans for welfare and not for evil, to give you a future and a hope." While this verse highlights God's faithfulness, many think it means God will prosper them by giving them a happy, successful life. This is not what Jeremiah was initially trying to communicate. The prophet Jeremiah wrote to the Jews who had been exiled to Babylon (Jer. 29:1). God was telling them to get comfortable in Babylon for seventy years (Jer. 29:5–70). That must have been hard to hear! After seventy years, He would fulfill His promise to bring them back to the promised land (Jer. 29:10). Then God tells them that He plans to prosper them (Jer. 29:11). He gave them hope that they would one day return to their home.

Although this verse is extremely popular, many people do not know that God had just punished the exiles for their idolatry by allowing Babylon to take them into captivity. They were receiving this message of hope in the pit of despair. God promised to restore them and rescue them from captivity. This verse shows Christians today the beauty and grace of God's heart. He constantly pursued Israel, although they turned their back on Him. Even in their darkest place and deep in the mess they made for themselves, God gave them a message of hope and future restoration. This verse does not mean we, as Christians, will always have it easy and good. It does not mean we will always be healthy or have financial security. Instead, this verse teaches us that even when we turn our backs against God, He is constantly faithful and full of grace.

As I said earlier, genuinely understanding Scripture takes work. Let's now look at tools that can help us interpret (understand the meaning of) and exegete (draw out the intended meaning of) Scripture.

A—Assess the Main Idea

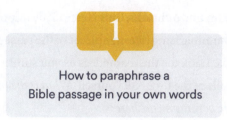

The first step in *A—Assessing the Main Idea* is paraphrasing. Writing out Scripture in my own words was one of the first Bible study tools I started with when I began reading Scripture years ago. I read one chapter each morning and then wrote a summary in my journal. That's it. For me, that was the best way to start learning how to study my Bible because it was challenging yet simple.

Paraphrasing recaps what you read and learned as you read it. Although this can be a difficult step in the interpretation process, it is vital because it requires reading for detail and meaning. If you want to truly understand a passage and assess the main idea, paraphrasing is critical. It is a priceless tool in Bible study because it forces the reader to understand the passage for themselves. It's easy to simply read the Bible, but much more challenging to put it in your own words.

Steps for Paraphrasing

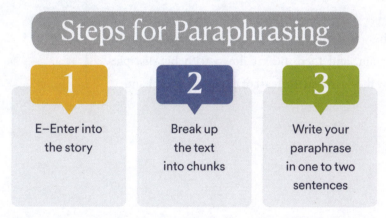

1. E—Enter into the Story. Ensure you have followed the observation steps in chapter 1. Read the text slowly to understand it fully.

2. Break up the text into chunks. This is especially important when reading a large text. Start by summarizing bite-size pieces of the passage and putting them into your own words. Look for the main ideas as you summarize, and leave out the more minor details of the text. Ask yourself: *What is the most important thing the author is trying to communicate here?*

3. Write your paraphrase in one to two sentences. Do not overdo it. Take off the pressure to add every detail to your summary. Stay simple by paraphrasing it into a few sentences.

TAKE ACTION Let's summarize John 6:1–15 about Jesus feeding the 5,000. We have already entered into the story and observed the text. Below, I have split the story into chunks. Summarize each chunk into one sentence. First, try this on your own, then look at my example to check your work.

John 6:1–15

1 After this Jesus went away to the other side of the Sea of Galilee, which is the Sea of Tiberias. 2 And a large crowd was following him, because they saw the signs that he was doing on the sick. 3 Jesus went up on the mountain, and there he sat down with his disciples. 4 Now the Passover, the feast of the Jews, was at hand.

A—Assess the Main Idea

5 Lifting up his eyes, then, and seeing that a large crowd was coming toward him, Jesus said to Philip, "Where are we to buy bread, so that these people may eat?" 6 He said this to test him, for he himself knew what he would do. 7 Philip answered him, "Two hundred denarii worth of bread would not be enough for each of them to get a little." 8 One of his disciples, Andrew, Simon Peter's brother, said to him, 9 "There is a boy here who has five barley loaves and two fish, but what are they for so many?" 10 Jesus said, "Have the people sit down." Now there was much grass in the place. So the men sat down, about five thousand in number.

11 Jesus then took the loaves, and when he had given thanks, he distributed them to those who were seated. So also the fish, as much as they wanted. 12 And when they had eaten their fill, he told his disciples, "Gather up the leftover fragments, that nothing may be lost." 13 So they gathered them up and filled twelve baskets with fragments from the five barley loaves left by those who had eaten.

14 When the people saw the sign that he had done, they said, "This is indeed the Prophet who is to come into the world!" 15 Perceiving then that they were about to come and take him by force to make him king, Jesus withdrew again to the mountain by himself.

THE EASY BIBLE STUDY METHOD

John 6:1–15

1 After this Jesus went away to the other side of the Sea of Galilee, which is the Sea of Tiberias. 2 And a large crowd was following him, because they saw the signs that he was doing on the sick. 3 Jesus went up on the mountain, and there he sat down with his disciples. 4 Now the Passover, the feast of the Jews, was at hand.

Context of the passage

5 Lifting up his eyes, then, and seeing that a large crowd was coming toward him, Jesus said to Philip, "Where are we to buy bread, so that these people may eat?" 6 He said this to test him, for he himself knew what he would do. 7 Philip answered him, "Two hundred denarii worth of bread would not be enough for each of them to get a little." 8 One of his disciples, Andrew, Simon Peter's brother, said to him, 9 "There is a boy here who has five barley loaves and two fish, but what are they for so many?" 10 Jesus said, "Have the people sit down." Now there was much grass in the place. So the men sat down, about five thousand in number.

Jesus tests His disciples' faith

11 Jesus then took the loaves, and when he had given thanks, he distributed them to those who were seated. So also the fish, as much as they wanted. 12 And when they had eaten their fill, he told his disciples, "Gather up the leftover fragments, that nothing may be lost." 13 So they gathered them up and filled twelve baskets with fragments from the five barley loaves left by those who had eaten.

Jesus performs a miracle feeding 5,000 with just a few loaves of bread and fish

14 When the people saw the sign that he had done, they said, "This is indeed the Prophet who is to come into the world!" **15** Perceiving then that they were about to come and take him by force to make him king, Jesus withdrew again to the mountain by himself.

} The people see Jesus is sent from God and want Him to fit their own agenda

Now, paraphrase the entire passage into one to two sentences. Think about this question as you summarize: *What is the most important thing the author is trying to communicate?* Try to complete this step on your own before looking at my answer.

Paraphrase John 6:1–15:

_____

_____

_____

Ashley's Insights

Jesus performs a miracle, feeding 5,000 people. The people perceive that Jesus is sent from God and desire to make Him king by force.

2

How to annotate
(identifying keywords and themes)

DIG DEEPER My high school teachers constantly had our class annotate when reading. Annotating is when you add notes, highlights, comments, summaries, and symbols to clarify the text, capture big ideas, and make it easier to review later. In one of my classes, the teacher hand-checked every page of our books to ensure we were doing the

THE EASY BIBLE STUDY METHOD

assigned reading and annotating. (Kind of intense, if you ask me!) From here, I took what I learned in high school and applied it to Bible study.

Annotating is a skill that can help you better understand and engage with the biblical text. You can do this in the margins of your Bible or a separate notebook. Everyone will have their own way of annotating; there is no "right" way. There is no pressure to annotate how I do or a friend does.

> **Mentor Mama Ellen Note**
>
> *If annotating feels overwhelming to you and you have an artistic flair, get creative! Feel free to highlight key points that are particularly meaningful to you through drawing, painting, or other art forms in the margin of your Bible or in a notebook. Artistic Bible journaling can help you express your thoughts and be an intimate way of connecting with God and impressing Scripture's message into your heart.*

Eventually, you will create a pattern of annotating that works for you.

Here are a few annotating tips and ideas you can do in your Bible:

- **Highlight or circle keywords and phrases.** Some questions to consider here are:
  - What keywords or phrases stand out to you as important throughout the text?
  - What words are repeated over and over again? These are important!
  - What does the author try to emphasize?

- **Make notes of the context of the passage.** Some questions to consider here are:
  - Who is the author, and what is the audience? What is their situation?
  - What is the genre?
  - Who are the main characters, and what can you learn about them?
  - Are there any geographical locations mentioned? Look them up in the biblical map (provided in the appendix). Many Bibles have maps in their appendix. Study Bibles and commentaries also have maps. Sometimes, I also search online for Bible maps. I will usually google

the location along with the Scripture reference and then look through the different photos on Google.

- **Mark questions.** What is confusing to you? Put a question mark next to it. Ask a trusted mentor or pastor about this or research it online and in commentaries.

- **Define words.** Look up words you don't understand and write down their definitions. How does the definition add to your understanding? You can look up the definition in an ordinary dictionary or a Bible dictionary, which may have a more precise meaning to the context of the passage you are reading. Do any of the words have a different meaning in the original context/culture? You can look them up in a Bible dictionary.

- **Connect ideas.** Each book of the Bible also has many other themes that are gradually unpacked throughout the book. What themes show up throughout the entire book you are reading? Additional key themes to look for throughout Scripture are love, redemption, justice, righteousness, grace, faith, obedience, suffering, joy, evil, brokenness, and sin. You can note these themes and connect them with a line or specific color.

- **Write out your prayers.** Take time to write your prayers in the margins. Write down whatever God is speaking to you. Talk with Him as you read.

- **Write down your honest thoughts.** No one will judge your annotations, so write honest thoughts about the text.

- **Look for God and His character.** God is the central theme of Scripture (we will learn more about this in chapter 3). When reading the Bible, I always look for God in a passage and what the passage says about who He is.

KEY THEMES WITHIN SCRIPTURE

- love
- redemption
- justice
- righteousness
- grace
- faith
- obedience
- suffering
- joy
- evil, brokenness, sin

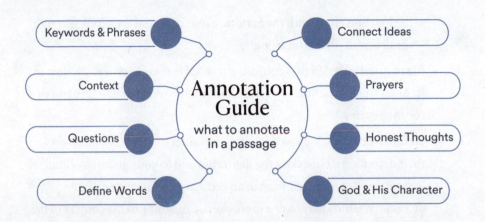

TAKE ACTION If you annotate while reading, assessing the text's central idea will be easier because you will have already noted key points and themes throughout the passage. Annotating is an excellent step toward finding the main point of a passage and understanding what is going on within any passage of the Bible.

We have been reading John 6:1–15 about Jesus feeding the 5,000. We will look within this passage again, but this time, we will take specific annotations to help us assess the main idea. Here is what I want you to look for and make notes of as you read through John 6:1–15:

- What is the previous context? What happens in John 5? (We looked into this already in chapter 1.)
- What locations are mentioned? Can you find them on the map that is provided in the appendix?
- Write the definitions for *Passover* and *denarii* (as we have already discussed in chapter 1).
- Who are the main characters mentioned in this story? What can you learn about them?
- What themes stand out to you?

Try this for yourself in the text below, then compare my notes with yours to expand your annotations.

A—Assess the Main Idea

John 6:1–15

1 After this Jesus went away to the other side of the Sea of Galilee, which is the Sea of Tiberias. 2 And a large crowd was following him, because they saw the signs that he was doing on the sick. 3 Jesus went up on the mountain, and there he sat down with his disciples. 4 Now the Passover, the feast of the Jews, was at hand.

5 Lifting up his eyes, then, and seeing that a large crowd was coming toward him, Jesus said to Philip, "Where are we to buy bread, so that these people may eat?" 6 He said this to test him, for he himself knew what he would do. 7 Philip answered him, "Two hundred denarii worth of bread would not be enough for each of them to get a little." 8 One of his disciples, Andrew, Simon Peter's brother, said to him, 9 "There is a boy here who has five barley loaves and two fish, but what are they for so many?" 10 Jesus said, "Have the

people sit down." Now there was much grass in the place. So the men sat down, about five thousand in number.

11 Jesus then took the loaves, and when he had given thanks, he distributed them to those who were seated. So also the fish, as much as they wanted. 12 And when they had eaten their fill, he told his disciples, "Gather up the leftover fragments, that nothing may be lost." 13 So they gathered them up and filled twelve baskets with fragments from the five barley loaves left by those who had eaten.

14 When the people saw the sign that he had done, they said, "This is indeed the Prophet who is to come into the world!" 15 Perceiving then that they were about to come and take him by force to make him king, Jesus withdrew again to the mountain by himself.

A—Assess the Main Idea

John 6:1–15

Previous context: Jesus heals the invalid. Jews are upset that Jesus heals on the Sabbath and is making Himself equal with God. Jesus confronts their unbelief.

1 After this Jesus went away to the other side of the Sea of Galilee, which is the Sea of Tiberias. **2** And a large crowd was following him, because they saw the signs that he was doing on the sick. **3** Jesus went up on the mountain, and there he sat down with his disciples. **4** Now the Passover, the feast of the Jews, was at hand.

location: Sea of Galilee

Common theme in John: Signs— Jesus performed signs (miracles). Many people were more enthralled by the signs than Jesus Himself.

Characters:
• Jesus
• Disciples — Andrew and Philip
• Large crowd— 5,000 "the people"

Cultural Word: Passover— The Israelites remembered how God redeemed them from slavery in Egypt.

5 Lifting up his eyes, then, and seeing that a large crowd was coming toward him, Jesus said to Philip, "Where are we to buy bread, so that these people may eat?" **6** He said this to test him, for he himself knew what he would do. **7** Philip answered him, "Two hundred denarii worth of bread would not be enough for each of them to get a little." **8** One of his disciples, Andrew, Simon Peter's brother, said to him, **9** "There is a boy here who has five barley loaves and two fish, but what are they for so many?" **10** Jesus said, "Have the

A denarius was a day's wage for a laborer. Perhaps this is thousands of dollars in today's money

Theme: Faith— Jesus is testing His disciples' faith

77

THE EASY BIBLE STUDY METHOD

people sit down." Now there was much grass in the place. So the men sat down, about five thousand in number.

11 Jesus then took the loaves, and when he had given thanks, he distributed them to those who were seated. So also the fish, as much as they wanted. **12** And when they had eaten their fill, he told his disciples, "Gather up the leftover fragments, that nothing may be lost." **13** So they gathered them up and filled twelve baskets with fragments from the five barley loaves left by those who had eaten.

Jesus:
God of
abundance

• Provider—
  physical needs
• Miracle worker
• Giver—of more
  than we can
  think or imagine

14 When the people saw the sign that he had done, they said, "This is indeed the Prophet who is to come into the world!" **15** Perceiving then that they were about to come and take him by force to make him king, Jesus withdrew again to the mountain by himself.

The people don't
fully understand
who Jesus is.
They may want
Jesus for their
agenda rather
than what Jesus
truly came for:
to save them
from their sins.

A—Assess the Main Idea

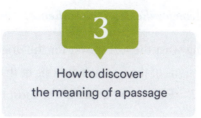

DIG DEEPER   Now that we have paraphrased and annotated the passage, we are ready to assess the author's main idea and conclude its meaning.

Finding the meaning of a passage can sometimes be challenging. It is important to remember that *we are not trying to discover a new meaning of the text* but rather to find what the original biblical author intended when writing to learn what that means for us today. This is not something we can do on our own. We need God to reveal the meaning of the text to us (Ps. 119:18; John 14:26; Eph. 1:17–18; Luke 24:45). Before interpreting Scripture, we must set ourselves aside and ask for God's guidance in our Bible study time. Only He can soften our hearts and open our eyes to understand His words.

> **Psalm 119:18**
>
> Open my eyes that I may behold wondrous things out of Your law.

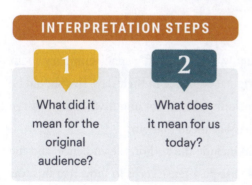

It is always important to remember that each book of the Bible has an original author and audience with a particular cultural situation. **Although the Bible wasn't originally written to us, there will always be truth that is for us.** When interpreting Scripture, there are two primary questions we can ask and look into: *What did it mean for the original audience? And what does it mean for us today?*

The Easy Bible Study Method

What Did the Text Mean for the Original Audience?

When considering what the text meant for the original audience, we first have to make observations of the text. We did this in the first step of the EASY Bible Study method, *E—Enter into the Story.* The most important questions to ask here are:

- Who is the author?
- Who is the audience?
- What is their unique situation, or what needs did the audience have that the author was trying to meet?

TAKE ACTION We will continue looking into John 6:1–15. Write a small one-sentence summary of the author, the audience, and the unique situation of John's audience:

_____

_____

Ashley's Insights

John writes to Jews and Gentiles, urging them to believe in Christ as the Messiah and Son of God.

After observing the text thoroughly, you can craft a small summary about what it specifically meant for the original audience in their day. This should be specific to the original audience, meaning this is not about what the passage means to you; rather, what did this passage mean to them?

Write a few small sentences that include the author, the audience, and the author's goal in writing. You can also use past-tense verbs to show that this was specific to them. What did John 6:1–15 mean for the original audience? Finish the sentence on the next page:

A—Assess the Main Idea

John shared with his audience . . .

> **Ashley's Insights**
> **John shared** with **his audience** the sign of Jesus feeding the 5,000.
> Through this, he **challenged** them **to believe in Jesus** as the Messiah.
> Although Jesus may not have fulfilled the earthly kingship the Jews
> desired, He came to seek and save the lost, which was His true mission.

In my example, I briefly summarized what this passage meant for John's original audience. As interpreters, it is our job to figure out what a particular author meant when he said it in his context and why. We can then use this as a springboard to discuss what the text means for us today.

What Does the Text Mean for Us Today?

After figuring out what the text meant in the original audience's day, we can now see what it means for us in our day. It is helpful to ask this question: *What differences and similarities do we share with the original audience?* You can quickly create two bullet point lists of the differences and similarities. Here are a few examples of what to look for when it comes to differences and similarities.

> **DIFFERENCES**
>
> - Cultural
> - Situational
> - Audience
> - Covenant

Differences

- *Cultural differences:* You live in a very different cultural setting than the people did in the Old and New Testaments. Cultural differences include language, food, social norms, clothing, values, politics, technology, and beliefs.

The Easy Bible Study Method

- *Situational differences:* Your current life situation may look completely different from that of the people found in the Bible passage. For example, Jesus was testing His disciples in John 6 to see if they had faith in Him to provide food for the people. He may be testing your faith, too, but it may look different. Perhaps He is testing you to see if you trust Him to provide a job you love and enough monthly income to pay off your school debt.

- *Audience differences:* Most of the Old Testament was originally written to the Israelites at different times in their history, such as Nehemiah, written for the post-exilic Jewish people recounting the rebuilding of Jerusalem's walls after they returned from captivity in Babylon. Much of the New Testament was written to early Christians and churches in the Eastern world, including Jews, Greeks, and Romans. Some books even have a specific recipient, such as 1 Timothy, which is a personal letter written by Paul to Timothy, helping guide him in pastoral leadership.

- *Covenant differences:* When you read the Old Testament, you are reading about the old covenant, which God set in place for the Israelites before Jesus came. As believers in Jesus Christ, we now live under the new covenant that Jesus ushered in. This is a big difference between how you and the original audience related to God. More to come on this later.

TAKE ACTION Within John 6:1–15, what differences do you have with the original audience? Note them here:

....

....

Ashley's Insights
Cultural

In John 6, John mainly writes to the Jewish people. I am not Jewish. I do not celebrate Passover, and I have not experienced life and culture as a

Jew. Therefore, that is a big difference for me to consider. I am a woman living in America, 2,000 years later.

Situational

In John 6, I am not in a situation where I have followed Jesus with a crowd of over 5,000 people and am now physically hungry. I am also not in the position of the disciples stressing over how they will feed and care for all these people. I struggle to relate with the Jewish people who were waiting for a king to overthrow the Romans.

Similarities

- *God.* He is always the same; He never changes. His character and attributes will always remain the same.
- *Sin.* All of humanity will struggle against the grip of sin until Jesus returns.
- *Faith, belief, and obedience.* Those who believe are all called to have faith and obey. This is a hard calling to follow in a broken world, no matter your generation.
- *Holiness.* All who believe are called to holiness and righteousness. We are called to reflect God.
- *Suffering.* All people will go through many different sufferings and trials in life.
- *Love.* All believers are called to love God and love people.
- *Redemption.* God offers redemption to anyone who will put their trust in Him.
- *Cultural or situational.* There may be ways you can relate to the original audience based on your current situation. If you are in your younger years, you will find many similarities you share with the original audience of Proverbs. Solomon wrote "to give prudence to the simple, knowledge and discretion to the youth" (Prov. 1:4).

TAKE ACTION Within John 6:1–15, what similarities do you have with the original audience? Note them here:

Ashley's Insights

Faith

Just like the disciples, I can lack faith. Jesus constantly "tests" my faith in Him through different life circumstances.

God

We love and serve a miracle-working God who continues to work miracles today. He provides in ways we could never dream or imagine. Jesus is a powerful and compassionate God.

Belief and Love

Many Christians may want Jesus for what He can offer rather than truly believing in Jesus and loving Jesus for who He is.

Jesus' Kingdom

Jesus inaugurated His Kingdom, which is also here today. We live under Jesus' reign as King and follow His ways above all else.

Now that you have assessed the main differences and similarities, you can conclude what the text means to you. Although you may not be culturally Jewish and are a Christian living 2,000 years later, this text has meaning for you today too. Write a small summary of what this text means for all believers. Use the similarities you found to help you craft your summary.

John 6:1–15 calls all believers to . . .

Ashley's Insights

John 6:1–15 calls all believers to put their weak faith in Jesus Christ, to believe that He is a compassionate provider and miracle worker, and to trust His Kingdom ways over their own.

Seeking Help

DIG DEEPER You may be wondering what to do when you don't understand the meaning of a passage, even after trying all these steps. It's important to remember that it's okay not to understand everything. Even Bible scholars struggle at times to understand the meaning of specific passages. You are not alone. Some passages may be straightforward to interpret, while others will be more difficult. That is entirely normal. Do not be afraid to ask for help. There are a few places you can turn to for help when interpreting Scripture.

First, God can open your eyes to understand His Word when you study Scripture. As a believer, you have the Helper, the Holy Spirit, to teach you all things (John 14:26). When you struggle to understand passages, ask God to reveal what those verses mean.

Second, I've already mentioned using free online resources such as commentaries and Bible dictionaries and study Bibles as you read Scripture. They are meant for people like you and me who want to understand the Bible but may need help. Simply look up the passage you are studying and read about what the interpreter has to say. How do their conclusions help add to your thoughts about what the passage means?

Third, you can also ask a trusted pastor or mentor for help. Talking with others about Scripture can be very eye-opening. Humble yourself and ask for help.

THE EASY BIBLE STUDY METHOD

TAKE ACTION Use a commentary or study Bible to gain additional insight into John 6:1–15. Look up the passage and journal your thoughts here. What new things did you discover and learn?

_____

_____

_____

_____

Ashley's Insights

One of my favorite theologians to learn from is Grant Osborne. His commentaries are helpful to read as I study the Bible because he always mentions things I didn't think of and addresses my difficult questions. For John 6:1–15, I used his commentary *John: Verse by Verse*. A few of his thoughts stood out to me:

- **Jesus' feeding displays a beautiful theme.** "God taking care of his people and providing for their needs. In this sense, there is a theology of community here, with Jesus and his Father caring for their family."[6]

- **This miracle points back to the Old Testament.** "It looks backward and reproduces the manna in the wilderness (Exod 16) and the multiplication of loaves when Elisha fed a hundred with twenty loaves of bread in 2 Kings 4:42–44."[7]

- **The Jews wanted Jesus for their political desires.** "They thought only of the Messiah as the King who would repeat Moses' deliverance of Israel from the Egyptians by defeating

---

6. Grant R. Osborne, *John: Verse by Verse,* ed. Jeffrey Reimer et al., Osborne New Testament Commentaries (Lexham Press, 2018), 147.

7. Osborne, *John,* 146–47.

> the Romans. They saw in Jesus the warrior-Messiah who offered them the opportunity for liberation, and they were perfectly willing to force him to go along if necessary."[8]
>
> After reading this commentary, I gained more insights into the meaning of John 6. I especially learned about the Old Testament connections that were not initially apparent to me as I studied this passage. I also learned more about Jesus' mission as Messiah and why the Jews could not understand His unique mission.

When Reading the Old Testament

As we have been studying John 6:1–15, Jesus has been at the center. Because the gospel of John is in the New Testament, we expect this to be true. However, we should never forget as we interpret all of Scripture that Christ should always be at the center of our interpretation because the entire Bible—both the Old and the New Testament—points to Him (Luke 24:27; John 5:39–40).

Earlier, I mentioned that the Old Testament was written before Jesus' death and resurrection. The ancient Israelites had not yet experienced salvation through Jesus. They believed in God and lived in communion with Him by keeping their covenantal relationship with Him, which included obeying the Law and the sacrificial system. To atone for their sins or rid themselves of their sins, they sacrificed animals as their substitute for the penalty of sin, which was death. The blood of the animals would cleanse them so they could be holy and live with a holy God, along with obedience to the Law. This is called the Mosaic covenant, or **old covenant**.

As Christians, we now live in the **new covenant**. We believe Jesus is the way, the truth, and the life. It is only through Him that we can have a relationship with God the Father (John 14:6). All people, Jews and Gentiles, are now able to receive salvation through Jesus. Jesus washed away our sins with His blood. He is "the Lamb of God, who takes away the sin of the world!" (John 1:29). He died

---

8. Osborne, *John*, 151.

the death we deserved. He gave us life in Him. We live in light of His grace (the gift of salvation) based on what He has done, not our works.

Therefore, when interpreting the Old Testament, we need to view every Scripture passage in light of the overall storyline of the Bible and our identity as children of God through Christ's redemption. We are not bound to the Old Testament laws or regulations; we are living under the gospel of grace.

Mentor Mama Ellen Note

It may be tempting to skim through the Old Testament or skip it entirely. But I want to encourage you not to neglect it. The Old Testament is critical to understanding our need for a Savior. Even though I grew up in the church, it wasn't until my thirties that I understood the meaning of the sacrificial system in the Old Testament and was truly saved. I didn't see a need for Jesus until I understood that we can't be in the presence of our holy and perfect God unless a sacrifice had been made in exchange for our sin. Putting this in context with Christ providing the ultimate sacrifice for our sin is how God lifted the scales from my eyes to knowing Him. You, too, will see the significance of the Old Testament when you embrace it wholeheartedly.

OLD COVENANT

- Before Jesus
- Israel had a relationship with God through . . .
  - Obeying the Law
  - Sacrificial System— Blood of animals temporarily atoned for sin

NEW COVENANT

- Jesus started a new covenant through His death on the cross. He is the Lamb of God who takes away our sins
- Through Jesus, we can have a relationship with God the Father
- We live in His grace

A—Assess the Main Idea

Finding the Meaning of Old Testament Texts

Sometimes, it is easy to figure out the meaning of the text for the original audience and for modern readers. Other times, it can be much more difficult. Let's get into two examples of what it looks like to interpret two different types of Old Testament passages.

Example #1—Proverbs 3:29

Do not plan evil against your neighbor,

who dwells trustingly beside you.

What did this mean for the original audience?

Proverbs is wisdom literature that gives insights into living. It was likely written by King Solomon for the Israelite people. In it, Solomon encourages people who already believe in God to walk in God's ways.

The Israelite people were living under God's laws. In their law, specifically Leviticus 19:9–18, they were commanded to love their neighbors by leaving food for the poor, not stealing, lying, swearing, robbing, etc. It concludes with "you shall love your neighbor as yourself; I am the LORD" (Lev. 19:18b). Proverbs 3:29 is a simplified nugget of wisdom that reminds the Israelites to love their neighbor by not walking in evil.

What does this text mean for us today?

What does this proverb mean for modern-day believers? Does it still apply to us today even though we do not live under Old Testament laws? In light of what Jesus taught in the New Testament, this verse still applies today. This is the main thing we share in common with the ancient Israelites: the command to love God and love people. Jesus said in Matthew 22:37–40:

"You shall love the Lord your God with all your heart and with all your soul and with all your mind. This is the great and first commandment. And a second is like it: You shall love your neighbor as yourself. On these two commandments depend all the Law and the Prophets."

89

The entire Old Testament Law can be summarized in two command-ments: love God and love people. Jesus emphasized that this is still true in His Kingdom today.

The meaning for all believers is to love anyone by honoring them and respecting them with loving words and actions rather than turning against them in evil ways such as stealing, lying, cheating, etc. Believers should treat others how they would want to be treated.

Example #2—Leviticus 4:27–31

Now, let's look at Leviticus 4:27–31. This is a more complex passage to determine what it means for us today. Read it here:

> If anyone of the common people sins unintentionally in doing any one of the things that by the LORD's commandments ought not to be done, and realizes his guilt or the sin which he has committed is made known to him, he shall bring for his offering a goat, a female without blemish, for his sin which he has committed. And he shall lay his hand on the head of the sin offering and kill the sin offering in the place of burnt offering. And the priest shall take some of its blood with his finger and put it on the horns of the altar of burnt offering and pour out all the rest of its blood at the base of the altar. And all its fat he shall remove, as the fat is removed from the peace offerings, and the priest shall burn it on the altar for a pleasing aroma to the LORD. And the priest shall make atonement for him, and he shall be forgiven.

What did this mean for the original audience?

Leviticus is the third book of the Bible. It was written by Moses, Israel's leader. The Israelites had just been rescued from slavery in Egypt. They were receiving God's Law so that God could live among them. Leviticus is about God's role with His people and gives instructions for proper worship. Within the book, there is a significant emphasis on holiness—personal, priestly, and national.

At the end of the passage, we read that the priest would make *atonement* for the sinner by sacrificing an animal, and the sinner would be forgiven. Animals became *substitutes* or took the place of the people of Israel. Although the people deserved death, an animal died in their place. This is called *atonement*, when someone or something covers over someone's death.

As modern-day readers of Scripture, it is strange to think that animal sacrifices were a common and daily ritual for God's people. Not many of us can relate to taking a lamb to be killed before our eyes. But animal sacrifices were a very powerful symbol for the Israelites. They were a graphic reminder of God's justice and grace for them. These sacrifices clearly showed God's *justice* because God did not let their sin go unchecked or unpunished. However, they also showed God's *grace* because He was allowing an animal to die in the people's place; they didn't have to take upon themselves the death they deserved. Generally speaking, sacrifices and offerings "restored broken relationships between God and mankind and between men and women."[9]

ATONEMENT

Animals became substitutes (took the place) for the people of Israel. Although the people deserved death, an animal died in their place.
This is called atonement when someone or something covers over someone's death.

After learning this information, we can now put ourselves in the original audience's shoes and imagine what this text meant to them. It was a practical command set out by God through their law for anyone who sinned. God gave them instructions on how to atone for those sins through animal sacrifice so they could be forgiven.

What does this text mean for us today?

Ultimately, the sacrificial system could not permanently take away Israel's sins because they continually had to make sacrifices over and over again. But that was never its goal. It was a temporary means for Israel to deal with their sins and to live in God's presence.

---

9. E. E. Carpenter, "Sacrifices and Offerings in the OT," in *The International Standard Bible Encyclopedia*, rev. ed., ed. Geoffrey W. Bromiley (Wm. B. Eerdmans, 1979–88), 260.

God's plan was always for Jesus, the Son of God, to take away the sins of the world. Acts 2:23 says, "This Jesus, delivered up according to the definite plan and foreknowledge of God, you crucified and killed by the hands of lawless men." The sacrificial death of every animal pointed to a greater day when Christ would die once and for all, for "Christ had offered for all time a single sacrifice for sins . . . by a single offering he has perfected for all time those who are being sanctified" (Heb. 10:12–14). So, let's break down what this means for us today by focusing on the similarities and differences we share with the Israelites.

- **Similarities we share with the Israelites in Leviticus 4.** One thing we share in common with the Israelites in this passage is our sinful nature and how all people commit sins (even sins done unintentionally or by mistake). Both the Israelites and we have to deal with our sins in some way if we want to be in relationship with a holy God.

- **Differences we share with the Israelites in Leviticus 4.** What we do not share in common with them is the way we deal with our sins. The ancient Israelites were commanded to sacrifice animals to atone for their sins. We have Christ, who already atoned for our sins and did this once and for all.

- **What does the text mean for us today?** The meaning for believers today is that sin is serious, and if we want to be in relationship with a holy God, we must rely on Christ to be our sacrifice and substitute. We do not need to feel shame and guilt for our sins; we can rest in the grace of our Lord Jesus Christ who takes away our sins for those who believe in Him!

Conclusion

Friend, congratulations! You are already halfway through the process of learning how to study the Bible. We learned how to *Assess the Main Idea* of a Bible passage by annotating, paraphrasing, and discovering the meaning for both the original audience and us today. With practice, you can confidently assess the main idea of any text you study! In the next chapter, you will learn how to seek God and His character as you study the Bible. You can do it!

A—Assess the Main Idea

STEP TWO: **A – ASSESS THE MAIN IDEA**

Paraphrase the passage in your own words.

- o Break up the text into chunks for summarizing into bite-size pieces and then write out a 1–2 sentence paraphrase.
- o Ask yourself: what is the main idea of this passage?

DIG DEEPER

- Annotate the passage (identifying keywords and themes).
  - o Highlight or circle keywords and phrases, make notes of the context of the passage, ask questions, define words, connect ideas, write out your prayers, write down your honest thoughts, note God and His character.
- Discover the meaning of the passage:
  - o What did it mean for the original audience? Conclude in one sentence what the text meant for them in their day.
  - o What does it mean for us today? What are the differences and similarities you share with the original audience? Conclude in one sentence what the text means for us today.
- Seek help from commentaries if necessary.

Discussion Questions

To help you reflect on the chapter, here are optional discussion questions that you can discuss with a friend, mentor, or small group.

1. What stood out to you from chapter 2? Do you have any questions?

2. The Bible wasn't written directly to us but is 100 percent for us. What does this mean?

3. Proverbs 3:5–6, Philippians 4:13, Jeremiah 29:11, and Matthew 18:20 are commonly taken out of context. Choose one of these verses and read it within its context. What does the verse mean within its original context?

4. What was your paraphrase of John 6:1–15? Was it helpful to put the passage into your own words? Why or why not?

5. What do Psalm 119:18, John 14:26, Ephesians 1:17–18, and Luke 24:45 teach us about our need for God to reveal the meaning of the text to us?

6. Why is it important to first look at what the text meant for the original audience?

7. What did John 6:1–15 mean for the original audience? What does it mean for us today?

8. What is the difference between the old covenant and the new covenant?

9. How can we interpret any passage of Scripture in light of Christ's salvation?

CHAPTER THREE

S

Seek God and His Character

From Taylor

could only study for so long in my shoebox-sized dorm room. So, one sunny Saturday afternoon, I recruited my friend Margo[10] to study with me at a coffee shop. One of the perks of attending a Bible college in downtown Chicago is that there are endless places to go and study. As we walked down the streets of Old Town, I felt confident that I would finally plow through the backlog of homework I had from my Romans block class. (Spoiler alert: Absolutely nothing got done.)

Margo and I attempted four coffee shops—each with standing room only—making it apparent that everyone in the city had the same idea as us! Thankfully, the last coffee shop had one table left.

As we sat down in the comfy little booth with our lattés in hand, an older

---

10. Name changed.

gentleman decided to also sit in our booth. He was a little too close for comfort—so close that we could feel him breathing down our necks, unashamedly leaning over to see what books we were reading.

To make the situation worse, Margo and I are both extremely non-confrontational, so we awkwardly pretended to read for a solid ten minutes before I caved. I glanced at her feverishly, signaling her to look down at her cellphone. I texted, *Do you want me to ask him to move?*

As she started texting me back, I made awkward eye contact with the older gentleman. To my surprise, his demeanor was less intrusive than I first thought. His eyes reflected a loneliness, aching to be met with genuine conversation.

He pointed to my Romans textbook and said, "Ah, I see you're reading about Rome! I grew up in Rome, and those were some of the best years of my life. What has you interested in Rome?"

After this casual opener, my fear of him being a crazy stalker diminished significantly. I relaxed my shoulders as my heart warmed up to his soft smile.

"Actually, this is a commentary on the book of Romans in the Bible. Are you familiar with Romans, or the Bible for that matter?"

Little did I know what a can of worms I had just opened as we succumbed to our fate of getting absolutely no homework done. An hour of conversation began, filled with a long history of his personal beliefs and experience with religion.

He told us that he was Iranian and grew up overseas. During his college years, he moved to America and worked his way up in the business world. His mother and father were Bahá'í, and his grandmother was Muslim. His family tried to force him to adhere to their religion, which only made him want to rebel more. Ultimately, he found both religion and God to be divisive and made it his goal in life to be as "good" as he could be.

Margo and I were able to talk back and forth with him about the differences between the God of Christianity and the God of Islam. After a good twenty minutes, I shifted the conversation to present him with the gospel, which I felt needed to be prioritized before we went our separate ways. I shared the foundational principle that all people have sinned against a holy God. Before I could go any

S—Seek God and His Character

further, I noticed his brows furrowing and his eyes squinting with skepticism.

He turned to Margo and asked her opinion about all I had claimed. Not only did Margo confidently reply in agreement, but she further explained to him how deep the nature of sin goes. She shared that our sinful nature can be traced back to Adam and Eve, the first people ever created by God. From their original sin, every man and woman after the fall was separated from God. She did not shy away from sharing that God is the one who declares us to be guilty before Him and even sinful at birth.

At this point, his core beliefs about God and His character were exposed.

"Why would I want to believe in a God that says I am sinful from birth?" he questioned. "What God is so unjust that He would not give me a chance to prove my goodness? I am not like those sinful murderers out there. I am a good person. If God doesn't see that I am good, I don't want anything to do with Him."

He then brought up the topic of natural disasters and spent considerable time sharing his personal grief; he had been scarred from witnessing innocent lives lost in seemingly helpless circumstances. He continued, "Where is God? And if God exists, He is clearly uninterested in the injustice occurring on earth. I don't want a god who lets evil pass day after day on earth to be the one to judge me. I know I am good, and if that isn't enough for Him, then I don't want anything to do with Him."

It was clear that the message about sin had struck a nerve. This man was convinced through his experiences with religion and the current state of the world that God is divisive, unjust, uninterested, and even cruel. Because he thought all of these things about God, he declared himself to be the righteous judge of not only himself but also God and His character. As a result, he refused to read the Bible or attempt to know Christ.

> **RIGHTEOUS**
>
> A word used to describe those who live morally upright lives.

Through sharing our faith that day, Margo and I discovered just how powerful a person's thoughts about God and His character are in determining one's willingness to accept the gospel. The reality is that we all have developed our own ideas about who God is. Even well-meaning

Christians can assume things about God that are not found in Scripture. Our thoughts about God and ourselves significantly impact not only our acceptance of the gospel but our entire lives thereafter.

The same is true and essential for us to know when reading God's Word. None of us come to Scripture unbiased. The reality is that from our personal life experiences and cultures at large, we unknowingly bring presuppositions about God and who He is. But we must allow ourselves to be transformed by the renewing of our minds daily in Scripture (Rom. 12:2). We need to know who God *actually* is.

We want the truth of God's Word to ultimately triumph over our flawed assumptions and beliefs about who He is. The main goal of this section is to help you read through a passage and confidently know *who* God is. Essentially, in this segment of Bible study, we will be focusing on the character of God and how to find it from the information and clues of any passage and summarize your findings in the simple phrase: "God is _____."

What You Will Learn

The focus of this chapter is on how to safely extract the qualities and characteristics of God from Scripture. This is the third step of the EASY Bible Study Method, to *S—Seek God and His Character*. You will learn three things.

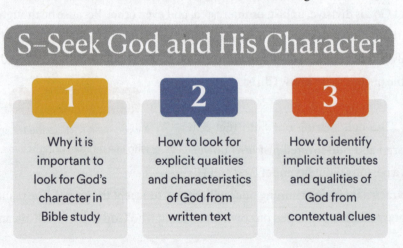

S—Seek God and His Character

1 Why it is important to look for God's character in Bible study

What does it mean to seek God's *character*? Character refers to qualities that are distinct to an individual. Think of the attributes that form one's traits, personality, nature, and temperament. In Colossians 1:15, Paul reminds us that Jesus Christ is "the image of the invisible God." In other words, Jesus is our ultimate knowledge of God! All we know about God's character is that which He has opened up to us in His self-revelation through His written Word (the Bible) and the Living Word (Jesus Christ).

So, we come to the Bible to learn firstly about who God is. That means that before we read Scripture with anticipation to immediately apply the text to ourselves (making us the primary object of our Bible time), we should read the text first to learn about God. One significant reason for this is that God is the central theme of Scripture. Throughout the Bible, God reveals who He is, how He loves, and ultimately, how He planned to redeem broken people back to His heart through Christ.

A. W. Tozer once said, "What comes into our minds when we think about God is the most important thing about us."[11] As image bearers of God, our identity is intrinsically linked to God. How we **think** about God significantly impacts how we **feel** about ourselves and **act**. It is psychologically proven that our thoughts affect our emotions, which in turn influence our decisions.

For instance, if you believe that God is impossible to please, you will likely feel anxious, fearful, and unsure of your salvation. These emotions will likely lead you to doubt, strive, and be apprehensive about coming to Him. Your feelings are dramatically affected by your personal view of God.

When we don't come to God's Word to understand who He is, we ultimately

---

11. A. W. Tozer, *The Knowledge of the Holy* (HarperOne, 1961), 1.

fill in the gaps of God's character with our limited life experiences and projections. If God is willing to tell us and show us who He is in the Bible, we shouldn't settle for a limited understanding of how great, powerful, and loving He truly is. We learn to grow and walk in the freedom of our faith when we become **confident** in who God is. Scripture is designed to assure us of His reliability and love for us; learning about the self-giving love of the Trinity will open our hearts to respond with feelings of love. As we learn about God, we can shed our old "understanding" of who He is to think rightly about who He is!

Mentor Mama Ellen Note

Before I started consistent Bible reading, I found myself praising God for the same things over and over again, like "My King" or "My Creator." Then, when I began soaking in God's Word, I realized just how much the Bible reveals about God! Now, when I study, I carefully review what I have learned about God each day and use it in my prayer time to praise Him. Give it a try, and you will see the breadth of the qualities of God to which He should be given glory, and that will increase your confidence and trust in Him!

SANCTIFICATION

The transformation that occurs when living like Christ causes us to look more like Christ.

We will become more *sanctified* in our walk with the Lord and even more conformed to the image of Christ. Therefore, as we learn to think rightly about who God is, we become more self-aware of who we are to live like! Jesus is to be our chief example of what our humanity should look like, as Scripture calls us to be like Him (Rom. 8:29)! When we understand more about who God is, we can begin to self-reflect and see how God wants to make us new, stripping off anything that hinders us from running the race of life like Christ (Heb. 12:1–2).

The Scriptures show us what transformed lives look like when people encounter the living God. They learn about who He is and, in fitting response, feel reverent fear, awe, joy, love, gratitude, worship, inspiration, and more. What we learn about

His character in Scripture will similarly shape our feelings. And, of course, when we are filled with love, gratitude, and reverent fear, we will act accordingly.

In the Bible, God changed every person who put their trust in Him. Jesus tells those who follow Him to *leave* their sin. Scripture tells believers to take up their cross and not be entangled by their sinful desires any longer (Matt. 16:24). However, it is not until we **know** and **trust** in God's character that we will be willing to live like this. Evidence of our trust in God's character will result in us bearing fruit (John 15:16). Our actions will be the outward evidence of our inward transformation. Our lives have to look different as a result of His resurrection power!

Two Things to Note

> **BEARING FRUIT**
>
> What happens when a heart changed by God produces outward actions

First, it is important to see God as triune (3-in-1). "God eternally exists as three persons, Father, Son, and Holy Spirit, and each person is fully God, and there is one God."[12] God as three persons is His primary attribute, and from this, all other qualities are informed.

As you read through Scripture, God will reveal Himself to you as Father, Son, and Spirit. Each person of the Trinity is fully God, but they are not each other; they each have unique roles and characteristics. God's triune nature can be found throughout the Bible, both in the Old and New Testaments. Yes, even the Old Testament can teach us attributes about Jesus and the Holy Spirit! While we will not delve deeper into the doctrine of the Trinity here, if you want to learn more, you should look into the book *Delighting in the Trinity* by Michael Reeves.

The second important note to remember when learning about God is that His character is unchanging. This means that the God He revealed Himself to be in Scripture over 2,000 years ago is the same God that He is today. What a beautiful truth to grow our faith! He is a God who is trustworthy, steady, and stable.

---

12. Wayne Grudem, *Systematic Theology: An Introduction to Biblical Doctrine* (Zondervan, 1994), 226.

EXPLICIT	**IMPLICIT**
• Is directly stated, no interpretation required • Does not require discernment to know	• Is not directly stated • Requires a level of discernment • Is found through context clues ○ Look to see what can be implied about God through actions, etc.

The Bible is filled with both explicit (plainly stated) and implicit (contextually implied) information about God and who He is. Christians throughout the centuries have relied on Scripture to form the basis of our knowledge about Him.

The main goal of this chapter is to help you read through a passage and confidently know *who* God is. Essentially, you can look at the facts and the clues from any passage and make conclusions about God's character. A simple way to summarize your findings is in the simple phrase: "God is (_____)."

2

How to look for explicit qualities and characteristics of God (from things plainly written)

Sometimes when you are reading Scripture, however, it will give you attributes of God that really stand out in one person of the Trinity. And since God is triune, there will be times that you will want to focus on the character of one particular person and attribute it to them. If the passage you are studying is talking specifically about one person of the Trinity, you can feel free to get specific by saying, "The Father is (_____)," "Jesus is (_____)," or "The Holy Spirit is (_____)."

When in doubt, you will never be wrong by using the simple phrase, "God is (_____)." This is because all three persons of the Trinity are fully God. Now let's begin by looking for the plainly stated qualities of God.

Look at John 13:13, where Jesus says, "You call me Teacher and Lord, and you are right, for so I am." This is an example of Jesus explicitly revealing Himself as a teacher and Lord. When seeking God's character in a verse like this, there should be no confusion about what Christ claims to be. We clearly see two traits:

- God is a **teacher**
- God is **Lord**

Other passages, like Psalm 103, explicitly show God as forgiving, healing, redeeming, loving, compassionate, satisfying, righteous, just, gracious, slow to anger, abounding in steadfast love, and more.

God loves to reveal Himself explicitly through His Word. You will not struggle to curate a list of attributes of God as you read both the Old Testament and the New Testament. One of the beautiful things about the character of God is that He is the same yesterday, today, and for all eternity.

TAKE ACTION Find explicit characteristics of God on your own. In Exodus 34:6, God reveals Himself to Moses. Read this verse and highlight the qualities of God. Then, write down these characteristics in the form, "God is _____."

"The LORD passed before him and proclaimed, 'The LORD, the LORD, a God merciful and gracious, slow to anger, and abounding in steadfast love and faithfulness...'"

God is...

- God is _____.

- God is _____.

- God is _____.

- God is _____.

- God is _____.

Once you have done this, you can check your answers by looking at mine.

> **Taylor's Insights**
> - God is **merciful**.
> - God is **gracious**.
> - God is **slow to anger**.
> - God is **abounding in steadfast love**.
> - God is **faithful**.

Knowing God's attributes can transform the way we think about Him. For instance, let's focus on God's attribute of being "slow to anger."

If we **believe** that God is slow to anger, we will be less likely to fear that He will snap at us, turn His back on us, or condemn us harshly. Our **feelings** about God will turn to trust and safety rather than fear. As a result of knowing this truth, our **actions** will likely look like drawing close to Him rather than running away. Knowing *who* God is changes the way that we live.

How to identify implicit qualities and characteristics of God (from things based on context clues)

Have you ever heard the phrase, "Actions speak louder than words"? There is truth to that! The Bible leaves room for truths to be found not only through explicit statements but also through subtleties. Implicit information about God can be suggested and understood through both the immediate and larger context of Scripture.

The Bible is nuanced, just like every good piece of literature. While writers share some things explicitly with readers, other times, their message is best given and received subtly, implicitly, and through contextual clues.

The characteristics not directly stated in passages can be found from context clues. For example, we can often make conclusions **based on the character's actions**. We see this in Psalm 56:3 when David says, "But when I am afraid, I put my trust in you" (NLT). When David is scared, he **chooses** to trust in God because of *who* God is. We can rightly conclude that "God is **trustworthy.**" And just like David, when we begin to fear, we can remember that God is always trustworthy.

We can also make inferences based on God's actions. In Psalm 56:8, David says, "You keep track of all my sorrows. You have collected all my tears in your bottle" (NLT). Looking at the actions of God, we would be right to conclude that "God is **caring**" or "God is **attentive.**" And just like God was caring and attentive to David, we can be sure He is the same for us too!

In passages like these where the writer doesn't plainly state an attribute of God, we must try to look beyond the actions to see the *why* behind God's heart! In this chapter's Dig Deeper section, we will look at a few journaling prompts to help you assess His character.

If we ever get confused about whether our conclusion is right or wrong, we can remember that the Bible never contradicts itself on who God is. For instance, if God reveals Himself to be "slow to anger," as Exodus 34:6 claims, then we cannot rightly infer from any other passage that God is "quick to

Mentor Mama Ellen Note

In our fast-paced world and desires for instant gratification, it can be hard to slow down. But unless you do this for your quiet time with the Lord, you will miss out on what the Holy Spirit wants to teach you each day. Slowing down is especially hard for me, as I constantly like to be on the move and get things done. But I have found that when I make it a habit to wake up earlier than I would like and spend time with the Lord first thing in the morning, God uses that time to ground me and prepare me for the day ahead. He will do that for you too!

anger." **What God directly says about Himself should overrule any conclusion we make about Him.** If our conclusion about God cannot be found anywhere else in Scripture, that is a red flag. We should see repeated themes of God's character throughout the Bible.

Our brains are already hardwired to make inferences! Our minds love solving puzzles, taking shortcuts, and ultimately getting us to the necessary conclusions! You may find this easier to do than you think.

TAKE ACTION Let's practice making inferences by looking at John 6:1–15, the feeding of the 5,000. There are not many attributes about God stated explicitly (only one), so it is time to remember the timeless phrase, "Actions speak louder than words."

As you read through this passage *slowly*, highlight the past and present actions of Jesus. You can also ask yourself: *What are those around God saying about Him?* Highlight those things. Then, write down a list of His attributes using the phrase "God is _____."

1 After this Jesus went away to the other side of the Sea of Galilee, which is the Sea of Tiberias. **2** And a large crowd was following him, because they saw the signs that he was doing on the sick. **3** Jesus went up on the mountain, and there he sat down with his disciples. **4** Now the Passover, the feast of the Jews, was at hand. **5** Lifting up his eyes, then, and seeing that a large crowd was coming toward him, Jesus said to Philip, "Where are we to buy bread, so that these people may eat?" **6** He said this to test him, for he himself knew what he would do. **7** Philip answered him, "Two hundred denarii worth of bread would not be enough for each of them to get a little." **8** One of his disciples, Andrew, Simon Peter's brother, said to him, **9** "There is a boy here who has five barley loaves and two fish, but what are they for so many?" **10** Jesus said, "Have the people sit down." Now there was much grass in the place. So the men sat down, about five thousand in number. **11** Jesus then took the loaves, and when he had given thanks, he distributed them to those who were

S—Seek God and His Character

seated. So also the fish, as much as they wanted. **12** And when they had eaten their fill, he told his disciples, "Gather up the leftover fragments, that nothing may be lost." **13** So they gathered them up and filled twelve baskets with fragments from the five barley loaves left by those who had eaten. **14** When the people saw the sign that he had done, they said, "This is indeed the Prophet who is to come into the world!" **15** Perceiving then that they were about to come and take him by force to make him king, Jesus withdrew again to the mountain by himself.

God is . . .

- God is _____.

- God is _____.

- God is _____.

- God is _____.

- God is _____.

When you finish, you can compare your answers and highlights to mine. We may not have the same insights, but that is okay.

Taylor's Insights

1 After this Jesus went away to the other side of the Sea of Galilee, which is the Sea of Tiberias. **2** And a large crowd was following him, because they saw the signs that he was doing on the sick. **3** Jesus went up on the mountain, and there he sat down with his disciples. **4** Now the Passover, the feast of the Jews, was at hand. **5** Lifting up his eyes, then, and seeing that a large crowd was coming toward him, Jesus said to Philip, "Where are we to buy bread, so that these people may eat?" **6** He said this to test him, for he himself knew what he would do. **7** Philip answered him, "Two hundred denarii worth of bread would not be enough for each of them to get a little." **8** One of his disciples, Andrew, Simon Peter's brother, said to him, **9** "There is a boy here who has five barley loaves and two fish, but what are they for so many?" **10** Jesus said, "Have the people sit down." Now there was much grass in the place. So the men sat down, about five thousand in number. **11** Jesus then took the loaves, and when he had given thanks, he distributed them to those who were seated. So also the fish, as much as they wanted. **12** And when they had eaten their fill, he told his disciples, "Gather up the leftover fragments, that nothing may be lost." **13** So they gathered them up and filled twelve baskets with fragments from the five barley loaves left by those who had eaten. **14** When the people saw the sign that he had done, they said, "This is indeed the Prophet who is to come into the world!" **15** Perceiving then that they were about to come and take him by force to make him king, Jesus withdrew again to the mountain by himself.

- God is **a healer** (John 6:2).
  - The "signs" they refer to are about Jesus healing sick people supernaturally.
- God is **relational** (John 6:3).
  - Jesus takes time to sit and be present with His disciples.
- God is **all-knowing** (John 6:6).
  - Jesus tests His disciples, knowing their hearts, as seen throughout Scripture.
- God is **thankful** (John 6:11).
  - Jesus thanks the Father, demonstrating His love for Him and what it looks like to have a thankful heart.
- God is **a provider** (John 6:11).
  - Jesus provides people physically with the food they need to survive.
- God is **a miracle-worker** (John 6:14).
  - Jesus performed the sign of multiplying food, something only He could do in His infinite power.

S—Seek God and His Character

- Jesus is **a prophet** (John 6:14).
  - The people rightly conclude that Jesus is the prophet foretold since the Old Testament.
- God is **wise** (John 6:15).
  - Jesus perceives every human heart and knows what people intend to do before they do it.

DIG DEEPER One way you can begin to dig deeper into your relationship with God is by **meditating** on His character. Meditation is one of many spiritual disciplines that can enhance your walk with Christ. Meditation, in a Christian sense, does not mean that you are emptying your mind; rather, you are filling your mind with a specific truth that you want to ingrain into your heart.

Meditation can extend beyond your normal reading time into a dedicated space. This is where you can focus on one section of Scripture, ranging from a few words to a whole chapter.

If you want to choose to meditate on a characteristic of God, take your highlighted verses on God's character and consider one of the following options to meditate with:

- **Prayer:** Pray over the verses, focusing on praising God for who He is.
- **Journaling:** Write down your response to God's character through means of poetry, songwriting, a letter to God, or simple journal entry.
- **Art:** Meditate on Scripture and have it inspire a watercolor, collage, sketching, etc.
- **Worship:** Sing songs that proclaim the attributes you read about.

Taylor's Insights

I will meditate on God's character through prayer journaling. The specific character quality I will focus on is that He is my Provider.

109

> Jesus, You are the ultimate source of power and healing. You are my Provider when I am lacking. You are the source for my every need. When I am weak, I should look to You for strength. Help me remember that I am not alone in any struggle I face, and I have a Savior who can empathize with what it is like to live in a human body. As I struggle not to worry about my finances this coming season, help me remember that You provide. Help me to trust that You can get me through anything in YOUR strength!

Conclusion

You should now be able to seek God's character in any text you read confidently. Knowing God's character will serve as a powerful anchor in times of trouble, doubt, and trials. Each time you study Scripture and look for God's attributes, remember them throughout your day. Call on God powerfully in prayer by proclaiming His greatness!

I hope that spending time seeking God and His character opens your heart so that you can more clearly see who He is, what He has done, and what He will continue to do in your life. In the next chapter, you will learn how to *Yearn for a Heart Change and Deeper Intimacy with God* so you can apply what you learn to your life properly!

S—Seek God and His Character

STEP THREE: **S – SEEK GOD AND HIS CHARACTER**

Write out a list of who God is from the passage. **"God is _____"**

- Find explicit qualities and characteristics of God
  - Attributes plainly written in the text

- Find implicit qualities and characteristics of God
  - Look at the context clues, mainly actions, to find attributes not plainly stated

DIG DEEPER

Meditate on God's character through

- **Prayer:** Pray over the verses, focusing on praising God for who He is

- **Journaling:** Write down your own response to God's character through means of poetry, songwriting, a letter to God, or simple journal entry

- **Art:** Meditate on Scripture and have it inspire a watercolor, collage, sketching, etc.

- **Worship:** Sing songs that proclaim the attributes you read about

Discussion Questions

To help you reflect on the chapter, here are optional discussion questions that you can discuss with a friend, mentor, or small group.

1. What stood out to you from chapter 3? Do you have any questions?

2. What thoughts about God do you have that may not be biblically founded?

3. Have you noticed certain emotions follow from these thoughts?

4. Sometimes, you can pick up on attributes of God that are not explicitly stated but found contextually. How can you know that what you infer is correct?

5. What does the Trinity refer to?

6. Why is God's triune nature important to remember when studying the Bible?

7. What attribute of God have you experienced most profoundly from John 6:1–15 and why?

8. Based on John 6:1–15:

   - What action is God taking or not taking? Why? What does this mean for my life?

   - How have I seen God show up for me in this way in my life, or do I hope to see Him show up in the future?

   - What thoughts do I have about God that need to change based on what I learned?

9. How can you ensure that your Bible study time is not just another religious activity but a time to connect deeply with your Creator?

CHAPTER FOUR

Yearn for a Heart Change and Deeper Intimacy with God

From Taylor

I was an up-and-coming college senior with the world at my fingertips. With friend groups established, favorite classes scheduled, and a single room to relax in, I was not expecting a sudden and painful relationship breakup. But two weeks before my big debut back on campus, my long-distance boyfriend broke up with me. Suddenly, the person I had attached my heart to so fiercely was gone. My mind raced incessantly for weeks, fixated on why I wasn't enough, ruminating on my pain and apparent unlovability.

Little did I know then what God would teach me through the anxious, knotted stomachaches and lonely midnight prayers. I had become so used to the rhythm of receiving love from my boyfriend that I was no longer craving the love of God. I had put my boyfriend on a pedestal in my heart and expected him to fulfill all my longings to be loved, seen, cherished, and wanted. The pressure on him was too much. In those prayers, I found myself learning to detach from the first man I had ever given my heart to and return to my first True Love.

Not only did God pursue me through my sleepless night prayer sessions, but He also came to me most profoundly through the book of Hosea. This is where most of my heart healing began. I had not yet been willing to reflect honestly on my mistakes in idolizing my boyfriend. But in Hosea, God revealed to me the areas of my heart that I was blind to and also showed me who He was. In Hosea 2:19–20 God proclaims this to the adulterous believer:

> I will make you my wife forever, showing you righteousness and justice, unfailing love and compassion. I will be faithful to you and make you mine, and you will finally know me as the LORD. (NLT)

Hosea is a book in which God reveals Himself as a loving bridegroom, coming to take back His wife, Israel, from her love affairs with idols. This book boldly calls out believers for their willingness to leave behind their first love for idols. It also shows us that God is committed to pursuing His bride at all costs.

The Holy Spirit worked in my heart to show me that I was no different than the Israelites obsessing over the love and affection of their prized idols. Through the reading of Scripture, my heart changed to focus less on losing the love and affection of my former partner and more on the ways that God, my bridegroom, was calling me to return to Himself. I went from striving and trying to be loveable to resting in God's unconditional and perfect love.

Learning that I am the bride of Christ weakened my obsession with finding my worthiness and lovability in a man's eyes. I believe God needed to use that season of a breakup to redirect the affections of both my former boyfriend's heart and mine. Through the Holy Spirit's guidance and inspiration from the book of Hosea, I decided to commit my fall semester to an intentional time of singleness. I wasn't expecting or asking God to bring my boyfriend back into my life, although my heart never stopped caring for him.

I spent the semester implementing the lessons I was learning in Hosea by dedicating that time solely to the Lord, allowing Him to work on my heart and lead me deeper into love and commitment. This decision was easily one of the highlights of my senior year, allowing me to root myself firmly in my identity as Christ's bride before opening my heart back up to any man. I spent my evenings before bed praying on my knees and frequently meditating on Hosea. I grew in my intimacy with Christ because I opened my heart to be operated on by the text. The Spirit gripped me where my life intersected with the Israelites, and only then could I reflect on the state of my heart.

Before I knew it, the semester flew by. For the first time in what felt like forever, my ex and I reconnected. Over tea and hot chocolate, we talked about what God had taught us, how we were humbled, and if there was room for friendship. God slowly opened our hearts to learn to trust each other again, and He redeemed what we thought was lost forever. After rebuilding our friendship, we decided to date again, and we became witnesses to the redemptive love of God firsthand! Now, we are more committed to each other than ever before.

The Holy Spirit gave me the desire to yearn for a heart change during that season. My intimacy with God skyrocketed through the reading of His Word. In this chapter, I want to show you how you can also begin to let your convictions and promptings of the Spirit lead to healing and change in your life! This is where you begin to allow God's text to seep into every crevice of your life and reflect on the state of your heart.

What You Will Learn

So far, we have walked through how to *E—Enter into the Story*, *A—Assess the Main Idea*, and *S—Seek God and His Character*. The fourth step of the EASY Bible Study Method is *Y—Yearn for a Heart Change and Deeper Intimacy with God*. In this chapter, you will apply what you have learned to your life. The aim is to do this holistically by engaging the text with your heart (inward) and actions (outward). In this chapter, you will learn:

Y – Yearn for a Heart Change and Deeper Intimacy with Jesus

1
How to engage your heart and mind in transformation

2
How to pursue Spirit-led action

Before We Go Any Further

Before we go any further, it is very important to remember that **we apply Scripture out of a place of being fully loved by God, not to receive God's love**. This means we are not trying to be good people and follow biblical rules to win God's approval and favor. Rather, we desire to follow God's way *because* we know He fully loves us; thus, we aim to please Him in everything we do.

We cannot accumulate enough good works to prove ourselves worthy of His love. This should set you free from striving. He loves us simply because He is love. You don't have to prove yourself worthy of Him by trying to be perfect; He knows you cannot be. Let your application of the Bible come from a place of worship and humble dependence, knowing He loves you not for what you offer but for who you are in Him—His child.

> **LEGALISTIC**
> Describes someone who attempts to earn salvation through good works/moralism rather than by faith

So, rest assured, God is not upset at you if you struggle to apply the Bible to your life. We don't want you to be *legalistic* about following all the Bible's rules. Take a deep breath, and allow

Y—Yearn for a Heart Change and Deeper Intimacy with God

the work of the Holy Spirit to lead you gently in the transformative power of God's love. The source of power for our ability to change is from God and God alone! Our job is to abide in Him and follow the leading of the Holy Spirit (John 15:5).

How to engage your heart and mind in transformation

Change always starts on the inside. Do you remember in the last chapter when I said that our thoughts impact our feelings, which ultimately affect our actions? This is important to note when applying what we learned from the Bible. We are motivated to act when our thoughts and feelings align with God's. Yearning for a heart change and deeper intimacy with Christ is about taking time to **reflect inwardly** before we delve into change.

Not all Bible applications look like a three-step method to perfect living; most don't. But nearly all of them require us to become introspective and chew on the words of Scripture. Before we apply them practically, God wants to see our hearts moved by His Word.

This meditation on Scripture renews our minds and leads to a deeper love, appreciation, and intimacy with God. Yearning for a heart change means that we are eager to let Scripture shape our desires because we know that God's way is best; this means being honest about our thoughts and desires.

> **Mentor Mama Ellen Note**
>
> *Meditation is a practice that seems to be dying in our culture. But what if we truly embraced the act of deeply engaging our minds on a portion of Scripture for a prolonged period? When I let God's Word sink into my soul, I have found that the Holy Spirit uses it to convict, encourage, and comfort me. Meditating on the Bible leads me to prayer, asking God to renew my heart and change my ways, which can be a wonderful application of the text. You should give it a try!*

One of the most rewarding journeys is letting God's Word change how you **live**. I find the best way to start the application process is through introspection, particularly journaling or praying. Talking to God helps us slow down, reflect on things that need to change, and invite God to help us.

Below are guided questions to help you journal or pray through your Bible time. You do not need to go through all of these questions each time you study the Bible. Simply pick a few to reflect on to guide your time of journaling. The goal is to have these questions help you yearn for a heart change and create deeper intimacy with God. For more questions, see the Dig Deeper section.

10 Questions for Application of the Text

1. In what ways is the Holy Spirit convicting me that my heart needs to look more like God's?

2. How does my current way of thinking need to be challenged?

3. What emotions am I feeling (e.g., fear, anxiety, bitterness) that need to be acknowledged and surrendered?

4. Should I be more in awe of who God is and spend time praising Him for His character?

5. How can a mindset shift, based on the text, change how I go about my day?

6. What desires of my heart lead to sinful behavior that the text convicts me of?

7. What is the Spirit convicting me that I need to believe or not believe based on the text?

8. Is my heart resisting the text in any way? What am I struggling to believe and why?

9. What barriers or baggage keep me from accepting the truths in the passage?

10. How can my heart be softened based on the text? How would the humbling of my heart change how I go about my day?

Y—Yearn for a Heart Change and Deeper Intimacy with God

TAKE ACTION *Let's grow in intimacy with God by analyzing John 6:1–15 with our questions. Read the passage now and be aware of your thoughts and feelings as you read. Now, pick one of the journaling questions that stands out to you. Take time to answer it.*

Journaling Question:

_____

Answer:

_____

_____

_____

_____

_____

Taylor's Insights

Journaling Question:

Should I be more in awe of who God is and spend time praising Him for His character?

Answer:

Jesus, I know that I should be more in awe of You! Let me praise You now: Holy, holy, holy, is the Lord Almighty! You are worthy of all my praise and adoration. I am transfixed by Your power and drawn to Your lovingkindness. I praise You for seeing the broken and needy. I praise You that You love so tangibly. I praise You for meeting all of our needs. I praise You for Your ability to work out all things for the good of those who love You. Lord, help me never to forget how awesome You are!

The Easy Bible Study Method

Let's practice again with John 6:1–15. Pick another journaling question that stands out to you. Take time to answer it.

Journaling Question:

_____

Answer:

_____

_____

_____

_____

Taylor's Insights

Journaling Question:

What barriers or baggage keeps me from accepting the truths in the passage?

Answer:

A barrier that is keeping me from connecting with You is unbelief. Here is my prayer to You:

> Dear Jesus, I know that You know my heart and that I struggle to accept the truth in this passage. Thank You for not making me feel ashamed as I bring my unbelief to You. I struggle to believe You can perform miracles and want to reveal Yourself to me that way! I need You to show me in my everyday life that You are the same God now that You were in the Bible. Jesus, I believe—but help my unbelief! I don't want You to feel silent in my life. I will continue coming to Your Word daily to open my heart to what it tells me about You. I will not let my doubts keep me from hearing You speak.

Y—Yearn for a Heart Change and Deeper Intimacy with God

DIG DEEPER Here are some additional questions if you want more to help stir your heart into reflection and action. The more time you take to be prayerfully introspective, the better! God's Word is meant to be chewed on and transformative for your everyday life.

- Am I wrestling with unbelief? In what ways?
- Is the text challenging my current ways of thinking?
- Does this text show me that my perspective of God is too limited?
- Is my current mental state affecting how I engage with this text? Does the text encourage me to think a certain way in which I am struggling?
- Are my ways of thinking in alignment with God's Word? What lies might I need to challenge after encountering what I've learned?
- Does this text show that I must address or shift my understanding of God's character?
- Are my heart's desires in alignment with Scripture? What needs to happen for me to rein them under the Holy Spirit's control and guidance?
- How does my heart need to be reoriented?
- Do the circumstances in the text correspond to a life event I am currently navigating and could learn from?
- Can I relate to how the people in the text interact with God? If I don't relate but should, how could I change? If I do relate but shouldn't, what steps should I take to change?

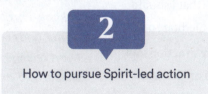

How to pursue Spirit-led action

Now that you have engaged with the text inwardly, it is time to make room for practical action. The Holy Spirit will take charge in this area, convicting or prompting you to *do* something about what you have learned. Sometimes, God will explicitly tell you what you should do in the text! Other times, you will reflect inwardly on the areas that need to be changed. Just learning about God's character will often move us to a place of conviction and repentance for the ways that we know we are not in alignment with Him.

Not all Scripture passages will lead you to a practical application point. That is because not every passage of Scripture was designed with this intent! Sometimes, the text is meant to magnify God's glory; in response, we can praise Him and be reflective. Other times, the text is more historical, such as lineage documentation or construction project directions and dimensions. These texts are great to learn from and engage in mentally and emotionally, but if you don't leave with a practical action-based application, your quiet time is no less valuable. In these cases, you can still grow in a deeper relationship with God by learning about Him and how He has worked through history to accomplish His purpose.

Here are some questions to lead you to a place of Spirit-led action:

- Does this text have explicit practical applications that I should follow?
- Does this text imply certain godly behaviors I should adopt as a believer?
- How can I look more like God? What practical steps can I take?
- Is this a passage that I should memorize and meditate on?
- How would love in action look in my life based on this text?
- Who should I be (or not be) based on the text?
- Is this text asking me to rest in His sufficiency rather than prove myself by good works?

Mentor Mama Ellen Note

Sometimes, I can feel the sting of God's Word being sharper than a two-edged sword. While applying these convictions often hurts, it's the only way I can change and grow to be more like Jesus. I like to share what I learn with someone who can hold me accountable, check up on me, and encourage me in the heart change process. Don't let shame hold you back from doing this too. You might just find it yields results a whole lot sooner!

Y—Yearn for a Heart Change and Deeper Intimacy with God

- How would my day look different if I modified the behavior leading me away from the Lord?
- Do I need to seek outside help or accountability to put into practice what the Holy Spirit convicts me of in the text?

TAKE ACTION Let's grow in intimacy with God by reading John 6:1–15 again and using our questions to help us create a practical action plan. After reading this passage, look through the questions you just read and be mindful about which one stands out to you in light of this passage. Allow the Holy Spirit to convict you and be open to adjusting your lifestyle to accommodate change.

Pick a journaling question and answer it.

Journaling Question:

Answer:

THE EASY BIBLE STUDY METHOD

Taylor's Insights

Journaling Question:

How can I look more like God? What practical steps can I take?

Answer:

Jesus, I am in awe of how You see people. As crowds of needy people approach You, You don't turn them away. At a moment's notice, You give Your resources freely. You do this knowing You will never get anything back in return. You give until everyone is completely satisfied. Jesus, I am convicted of the way that I use my resources selfishly. I complain about how little I have and hoard it all for me to use alone. I am constantly thinking about how I need to provide for myself and rarely ever how I can use my resources to bless others. Jesus, I will commit 10 percent of my income to tithe at church this Sunday. I know You have been stirring me to give You what is Yours. I also know how much You cherish the church and how You desire me to give freely to my church family. Jesus, I know that You will bless me as I give. Help me to be a cheerful giver.

DIG DEEPER One way to provide direction and accountability for your future actions is by creating goals. While not every application you make in Bible study will relate to a goal, many of your applications will. When done well, goals can provide a detailed outline of how you plan to change your life. This can easily be applied to your spiritual life; the sanctification journey requires intentional work on our part to partner with the Spirit in change.

A plan can help transform your idea of how you want to change into actionable steps. Goals should be created prayerfully, however. Proverbs 16:9 says, "The heart of man plans his way, but the LORD establishes his steps." Ask God to partner with you in your goals, and be willing to pivot if He puts something more pressing on your heart. Ask Him that you would only do what He wants for your life rather than assuming you are in total control. Submit all your ways to Him, and He will direct your path (Prov. 3:6).

Y—Yearn for a Heart Change and Deeper Intimacy with God

One way to create realistic goals for spiritual growth is by creating SMART goals. George T. Doran created this acronym tool, where each letter points to helpful criteria to make goals more likely to succeed.[13] The letters stand for Specific, Measurable, Achievable, Relevant, and Time-Bound. This acronym has helped thousands of people create realistic and attainable goals.

To create a SMART goal, start by writing down your initial goal. Then, walk through the five letters, answer the questions, and get as specific as you can; not every goal you create will have all five criteria. Once you are finished, rewrite your final goal as it has been tweaked. See the infographic to learn about each letter of the SMART goal.[14]

Initial Goal:

Specific	**Measurable**	**Achievable**	**Relevant**	**Time-Bound**
• Think about what you are trying to accomplish and why (get detailed). • Consider who may need to be involved if you'll need help. • What obstacles could get in your way?	• How will you measure your progress? • How will you determine when your goal is achieved?	• What do you need to do to make this goal happen? • Do you possess the skills needed, or have to outsource? • Is the amount of effort required worth your time?	• Does this goal align with your values? • Does this goal make sense for the stage of life that you are in?	• When do you hope to accomplish your goal? • Is your deadline realistic? • What milestone markers are needed if any?

Final Goal:

---

13. "A Brief History of SMART Goals," *Project Smart*, https://www.projectsmart.co.uk/smart-goals/brief-history-of-smart-goals.php.
14. Our infographic is inspired by University of California, *Smart Goals: A How to Guide*, https://www.ucop.edu/local-human-resources/_files/performance-appraisal/How+to+write+SMART+Goals+v2.pdf.

125

THE EASY BIBLE STUDY METHOD

TAKE ACTION Let's try this out by looking again at the passage from John we've been studying. Think about something practical that you want to change in your life based on the convictions you felt while reading this. It can be small or large, but just make sure it is something tangible to work on.

Write out your initial goal here:

_____

_____

_____

_____

Now, walk through each letter of the acronym by answering the questions provided in the infographic. This will help you clarify the steps you will need to take and if your goal needs adjusting!

Specific:

_____

_____

_____

_____

Measurable:

_____

_____

_____

_____

Y—Yearn for a Heart Change and Deeper Intimacy with God

Achievable:

Relevant:

Time-Bound:

Once you are finished, rewrite your refurbished goal below. (It can be brief, but it should be clearer than your initial goal.)

Taylor's Insights

As I read this passage, I was convicted about how Jesus selflessly provided for the crowd. He has always demonstrated what it looks like to give of oneself from a place of faith. I also want to be able to give from a place of faith, trusting that God will provide for me financially. My heart is stirred toward giving to the church.

Initial Goal:
My goal is to start tithing to the church regularly.

Specific:
I want to tithe 10 percent of my income. I want to do it electronically so that I don't have to remember to bring cash to church each week. Who might need to help? I will need to ask the church for assistance in creating an online account so that I can give weekly online.

Obstacles: I anticipate a lot of financial stress keeping me from trying to tithe; I will need to schedule a time on my calendar this week after work to budget and ensure I have the funds to prioritize this giving. I want to invite God into my giving and do it with a cheerful, not fearful, heart.

Measurable:
I will know I am making progress when I have established my online church account, connected it to my bank, and set it up for continued withdrawal. When those three things are completed, I will consider my goal achieved.

Achievable:
To make this happen, I will mark my calendar to call the church on Friday at noon to help me create an account and connect my bank. With the help of church staff, I will have the skills to make this happen. This is a small amount of effort and will be completely worth my time.

Relevant:

This goal perfectly aligns with my values. When I start tithing, I know that I will feel closer to the Lord in giving back to Him what is already His. While money will be tight at this stage of my life, I know it is still the right thing to do. I want to exercise trust and reliance on God to get me through.

Time-Bound:

I want to accomplish this goal by next week. This timeline is realistic, and I don't need milestone markers.

Refurbished Goal:

My goal is to tithe weekly. I will accomplish this goal next week by:

1. Setting up an appointment with the church for Friday at noon
2. Create my online account with my church and connect my bank account during the phone appointment.
3. Check my budget that weekend and ensure that I have the funds to tithe 10 percent.
4. Once budget is clear, set up automatic 10 percent withdrawals from my paycheck each week.

Conclusion

Applying God's Word to my life during my breakup completely transformed me. It gave me a deeper intimacy with God and hope to endure through the darkest nights. This experience showed me that God's Word is more than just a history book; engaging in the Bible is practical for daily life! Jesus says, "Whoever abides in me and I in him, he it is that bears much fruit, for apart from me you can do nothing" (John 15:5). Living our lives apart from God will bear us no fruit. But letting Him into our hearts and minds can transform us and bring us from surviving to thriving.

STEP FOUR: Y – YEARN FOR A HEART CHANGE AND DEEPER INTIMACY WITH GOD

Journaling questions for inward transformation of heart and mind

- In what ways is the Holy Spirit convicting me that my heart needs to look more like God's heart?
- How does my current way of thinking need tobe challenged?
- What emotions am I feeling (e.g., fear, anxiety, bitterness) that need to be acknowledged and surrendered?
- Should I be more in awe of who God is and spend time simply praising Him for His character?
- How can a mindset shift, based on the text, change how I go about my day?

Journaling questions for outward application

- Does this text have explicit practical applications that I should follow?
- Does this text imply certain godly behaviors I should adopt as a believer?
- How can I look more like God? What practical steps can I take?
- Is this a passage that I should memorize and meditate on?

DIG DEEPER

- Create SMART goals to help you achieve your intended outcome.

Discussion Questions

To help you reflect on the chapter, here are optional discussion questions that you can discuss with a friend, mentor, or small group.

1. What stood out to you from chapter 4? Do you have any questions?

2. How can you practically apply Scripture out of a place of being fully loved by God, not to receive God's love?

3. Why is it important that God's Word transforms both your heart (inward) and your actions (outward)?

4. Does the application of God's Word come naturally to you? Why or why not?

5. What obstacles do you foresee keeping you from applying God's Word practically to your life?

6. What would asking the Holy Spirit to partner with you in the sanctification process look like?

7. After studying John 6:1–15, in what areas (heart and actions) were you convicted?

8. Does it excite you to create SMART goals in your walk with God? What are the pros and cons of creating such detailed plans? Share your specific goal.

CHAPTER FIVE

Putting It All Together

From Ashley

Now, let's put the entire EASY Bible Study Method together by studying Exodus 16. This Old Testament passage parallels the John 6 passage we have been studying about Jesus feeding the 5,000.

For this study of Exodus 16, I will lead you through the EASY Bible Study Method. I will give you the opportunity to study the passage for yourself and then check your answers with mine. Let's get started!

E—Enter into the Story

STEP ONE: E – ENTER INTO THE STORY

- **Pray** before reading
- **Read** the text slowly and thoughtfully
- **Determine** the context
  - Where does this fit in the storyline of the Bible?
  - Who was the original author?
  - Who was the original audience and what were they going through?
- **Put** yourself in the story
- **Ask** good questions

THE EASY BIBLE STUDY METHOD

DIG DEEPER

- Read the text in different translations: ESV, NLT, NIV, NKJV
- When was this written? What was the date? What major events were going on during this time?
- Are there any historical or cultural things, customs, locations, or elements within the text that could be researched more in order to understand the meaning?
- What is the surrounding context of the verse or passage you are studying?
- What is the literary genre of this text and how does that add to the meaning of the passage?

Pray

Start your Bible study time with prayer. Feel free to write out your prayer here:

Ashley's Insights

Lord, teach me. I want to learn more about You and more about Your Word. I cannot understand without You. Please open my eyes so that You might be glorified through my Bible study time.

Read

Read Exodus 16 slowly and thoughtfully. If you desire, you can also listen to the text while reading. Journal any initial observations you have:

Putting It All Together

Ashley's Insights

I immediately noticed how much the Israelites complained and did not listen to Moses or God. It seems like such an incredible miracle, yet their selfishness so blinded the Israelites that they missed God's glory.

Determine the Context

Look for the answers in a commentary, study Bible, or online. As a reminder, check out our recommended resource guide for free online sources. You can find the QR code for that in chapter 1.

Where does this fit in the storyline of the Bible? Is it in creation, fall, redemption, or new creation?

Who is the author?

Who was the original audience, and what were they going through?

THE EASY BIBLE STUDY METHOD

Ashley's Insights

Where does this fit in the storyline of the Bible? Is it in creation, fall, redemption, or new creation?

This happens after the fall and before redemption. It is directly following the Israelites' salvation and exit from slavery in Egypt.

Who is the author?

Moses is known to have written Exodus. Moses was one of Israel's greatest leaders and prophets. God spoke to Moses directly and used Moses to lead Israel out of Egypt, through the wilderness for forty years, and toward the promised land.

Who was the original audience, and what were they going through?

Moses wrote Exodus to help the Israelite people remember how God had saved them from slavery in Egypt. He also wrote to instruct them on God's Law and their covenantal relationship with God.

Put Yourself in the Story

Reread Exodus 16. What would you have heard, tasted, smelled, saw, and felt if you were an Israelite in the story? How would you feel? What's the overall mood of this passage?

Putting It All Together

Ashley's Insights

As I put myself in the Israelites' shoes, I feel the weight of being in a wilderness away from any type of civilization and food that they were used to in Egypt. I would be afraid that my family or I would go hungry and die. I would struggle to trust God and perhaps be confused as to why He saved us from Egypt, and yet it feels like He isn't taking care of our basic needs now. I know it's easy to wonder why the Israelites grumbled, but I think I would have grumbled too. I am so prone to complain and whine.

If I were an Israelite in this situation, I hope I would have been filled with wonder and gratefulness toward God for revealing His glory and providing sweet bread in the wilderness. It didn't seem like the Israelites cared much.

I definitely can feel the stress and anger of Moses, who is called to lead a very stubborn group of people.

Ask Good Questions

As you read Exodus 16, what questions came up?

The Easy Bible Study Method

Ashley's Insights

- Why did the Israelites so easily forget about God's previous miracles and Him saving them from slavery?
- God said He would give them the bread to test them. What was this test?
- What did the manna look like? What was its consistency? How did they prepare it?
- Why were the Israelites stubborn, disobedient, and unaware of God's glory?

DIG DEEPER Read or listen to the text in different translations (ESV, NLT, NIV, NKJV). Did anything new stand out to you?

Ashley's Insights

- Desert (NIV), wilderness (ESV)
- This happened one month after leaving Egypt (Ex. 16:1 NLT and NIV).
- God is testing them to see if they will follow His instructions and Law, especially about the Sabbath (Ex. 16:4 NLT and ESV).
- Their complaints are against the Lord, not against Moses or Aaron (Ex. 16:7–8 NLT).
- "They must realize that the Sabbath is the LORD's gift to you" (Ex. 16:29 NLT).
- Manna literally means "What is it?"
- Goal: for them to know that God is the Lord their God (Ex. 16:12) and that He rescued them from slavery (Ex. 16:6).

Putting It All Together

When was this written?

Ashley's Insights

Many scholars believe this was written around 1,400 BC.

Define

Is there anything within the text that needs to be researched more fully, such as historical or cultural things, locations, events, or customs? If so, list and define these.

Ashley's Insights

- *Locations:* Elim, Wilderness of Sin, Sinai, Egypt, border of the land of Canaan
- *The glory of the LORD in the cloud:* A cloud by day and fire by night, a manifestation of God's presence in Exodus, leading and protecting His people
- *The camp:* Exodus 12:37 says there were about 600,000 men (not including women and children)
- *Quail:* A bird God provided for them in the wilderness to eat
- *Manna:* Manna literally means "What is it?"
- *Omer:* Two quarts or two liters
- *Sabbath:* "To cease" from work

THE EASY BIBLE STUDY METHOD

Literary Genre

What is the literary genre of the text?

Ashley's Insights

Historical Narrative: It recounts specific historical events from Israel's history in a story-like format.

A—Assess the Main Idea

STEP TWO: **A – ASSESS THE MAIN IDEA**

Paraphrase the passage in your own words.

- o Break up the text into chunks for summarizing into bite-size pieces and then write out a 1–2 sentence paraphrase.
- o Ask yourself: What is the main idea of this passage?

DIG DEEPER

- Annotate the passage (identifying keywords and themes).
- o Highlight or circle keywords and phrases, make notes of the context of the passage, ask questions, define words, connect ideas, write out your prayers, write down your honest thoughts, note God and His character.

- Discover the meaning of the passage:
  - What did it mean for the original audience? Conclude in one sentence what the text meant for them in their day.
  - What does it mean for us today? What are the differences and similarities you share with the original audience? Conclude in one sentence what the text means for us today.
- Seek help from commentaries if necessary.

Paraphrase

Paraphrase each chunk of the passage in your own words.

Exodus 16

1 They set out from Elim, and all the congregation of the people of Israel came to the wilderness of Sin, which is between Elim and Sinai, on the fifteenth day of the second month after they had departed from the land of Egypt. 2 And the whole congregation of the people of Israel grumbled against Moses and Aaron in the wilderness, 3 and the people of Israel said to them, "Would that we had died by the hand of the LORD in the land of Egypt, when we sat by the meat pots and ate bread to the full, for you have brought us out into this wilderness to kill this whole assembly with hunger."

4 Then the LORD said to Moses, "Behold, I am about to rain bread from heaven for you, and the people shall go out and gather a day's portion every day, that I may test them, whether they will walk in my law or not. **5** On the sixth day, when they prepare what they bring in, it will be twice as much as they gather daily." **6** So Moses and Aaron said to all the people of Israel, "At evening you shall know that it was the LORD who brought you out of the land of Egypt, **7** and in the morning you shall see the glory of the LORD, because he has heard your grumbling against the LORD. For what are we, that you grumble against us?" **8** And Moses said, "When the LORD gives you in the evening meat to eat and in the morning bread to the full, because the LORD has heard your grumbling that you grumble against him—what are we? Your grumbling is not against us but against the LORD."

9 Then Moses said to Aaron, "Say to the whole congregation of the people of Israel, 'Come near before the LORD, for he has heard your grumbling.'" **10** And as soon as Aaron spoke to the whole congregation of the people of Israel, they looked toward the wilderness, and behold, the glory of the LORD appeared in the cloud. **11** And the LORD said to Moses, **12** "I have heard the grumbling of the people of Israel. Say to them, 'At twilight you shall eat meat, and in the morning you shall be filled with bread. Then you shall know that I am the LORD your God.'"

Putting It All Together

13 In the evening quail came up and covered the camp, and in the morning dew lay around the camp. **14** And when the dew had gone up, there was on the face of the wilderness a fine, flake-like thing, fine as frost on the ground. **15** When the people of Israel saw it, they said to one another, "What is it?" For they did not know what it was. And Moses said to them, "It is the bread that the LORD has given you to eat. **16** This is what the LORD has commanded: 'Gather of it, each one of you, as much as he can eat. You shall each take an omer, according to the number of the persons that each of you has in his tent.'" **17** And the people of Israel did so. They gathered, some more, some less. **18** But when they measured it with an omer, whoever gathered much had nothing left over, and whoever gathered little had no lack. Each of them gathered as much as he could eat. **19** And Moses said to them, "Let no one leave any of it over till the morning." **20** But they did not listen to Moses. Some left part of it till the morning, and it bred worms and stank. And Moses was angry with them. **21** Morning by morning they gathered it, each as much as he could eat; but when the sun grew hot, it melted.

22 On the sixth day they gathered twice as much bread, two omers each. And when all the leaders of the congregation came and told Moses, 23 he said to them, "This is what the LORD has commanded: 'Tomorrow is a day of solemn rest, a holy Sabbath to the LORD; bake what you will bake and boil what you will boil, and all that is left over lay aside to be kept till the morning.'" 24 So they laid it aside till the morning, as Moses commanded them, and it did not stink, and there were no worms in it. 25 Moses said, "Eat it today, for today is a Sabbath to the LORD; today you will not find it in the field. 26 Six days you shall gather it, but on the seventh day, which is a Sabbath, there will be none."

27 On the seventh day some of the people went out to gather, but they found none. 28 And the LORD said to Moses, "How long will you refuse to keep my commandments and my laws? 29 See! The LORD has given you the Sabbath; therefore on the sixth day he gives you bread for two days. Remain each of you in his place; let no one go out of his place on the seventh day." 30 So the people rested on the seventh day.

Putting It All Together

31 Now the house of Israel called its name manna. It was like coriander seed, white, and the taste of it was like wafers made with honey. **32** Moses said, "This is what the LORD has commanded: 'Let an omer of it be kept throughout your generations, so that they may see the bread with which I fed you in the wilderness, when I brought you out of the land of Egypt.'" **33** And Moses said to Aaron, "Take a jar, and put an omer of manna in it, and place it before the LORD to be kept throughout your generations." **34** As the LORD commanded Moses, so Aaron placed it before the testimony to be kept. **35** The people of Israel ate the manna forty years, till they came to a habitable land. They ate the manna till they came to the border of the land of Canaan. **36** (An omer is the tenth part of an ephah.)

Ashley's Insights

Exodus 16

1 They set out from Elim, and all the congregation of the people of Israel came to the wilderness of Sin, which is between Elim and Sinai, on the fifteenth day of the second month after they had departed from the land of Egypt. **2** And the whole congregation of the people of Israel grumbled against Moses and Aaron in the wilderness, **3** and the people of Israel said to them, "Would that we had died by the hand of the LORD in the land of Egypt, when we sat by the meat pots and ate bread to the full, for you have brought us out into this wilderness to kill this whole assembly with hunger."

A month after the Passover, Israel came to the wilderness and complained to God about their hunger.

THE EASY BIBLE STUDY METHOD

4 Then the LORD said to Moses, "Behold, I am about to rain bread from heaven for you, and the people shall go out and gather a day's portion every day, that I may test them, whether they will walk in my law or not. 5 On the sixth day, when they prepare what they bring in, it will be twice as much as they gather daily." 6 So Moses and Aaron said to all the people of Israel, "At evening you shall know that it was the LORD who brought you out of the land of Egypt, 7 and in the morning you shall see the glory of the LORD, because he has heard your grumbling against the LORD. For what are we, that you grumble against us?" 8 And Moses said, "When the LORD gives you in the evening meat to eat and in the morning bread to the full, because the LORD has heard your grumbling that you grumble against him—what are we? Your grumbling is not against us but against the LORD."

> The LORD heard their grumbling that was against Him. So God said He would rain bread from heaven and the people were to follow His rules.

9 Then Moses said to Aaron, "Say to the whole congregation of the people of Israel, 'Come near before the LORD, for he has heard your grumbling.'" 10 And as soon as Aaron spoke to the whole congregation of the people of Israel, they looked toward the wilderness, and behold, the glory of the LORD appeared in the cloud. 11 And the LORD said to Moses, 12 "I have heard the grumbling of the people of Israel. Say to them, 'At twilight you shall eat meat, and in the morning you shall be filled with bread. Then you shall know that I am the LORD your God.'"

> The congregation assembled before the LORD who manifested His glory in a cloud.

Putting It All Together

13 In the evening quail came up and covered the camp, and in the morning dew lay around the camp. **14** And when the dew had gone up, there was on the face of the wilderness a fine, flake-like thing, fine as frost on the ground. **15** When the people of Israel saw it, they said to one another, "What is it?" For they did not know what it was. And Moses said to them, "It is the bread that the Lord has given you to eat. **16** This is what the Lord has commanded: 'Gather of it, each one of you, as much as he can eat. You shall each take an omer, according to the number of the persons that each of you has in his tent.'" **17** And the people of Israel did so. They gathered, some more, some less. **18** But when they measured it with an omer, whoever gathered much had nothing left over, and whoever gathered little had no lack. Each of them gathered as much as he could eat. **19** And Moses said to them, "Let no one leave any of it over till the morning." **20** But they did not listen to Moses. Some left part of it till the morning, and it bred worms and stank. And Moses was angry with them. **21** Morning by morning they gathered it, each as much as he could eat; but when the sun grew hot, it melted.

God gave meat (quail) in the evening and bread (manna) in the morning. The people gathered the manna, but some did not follow the rules. Morning by morning, God provided manna.

THE EASY BIBLE STUDY METHOD

22 On the sixth day they gathered twice as much bread, two omers each. And when all the leaders of the congregation came and told Moses, 23 he said to them, "This is what the LORD has commanded: 'Tomorrow is a day of solemn rest, a holy Sabbath to the LORD; bake what you will bake and boil what you will boil, and all that is left over lay aside to be kept till the morning.'" 24 So they laid it aside till the morning, as Moses commanded them, and it did not stink, and there were no worms in it. 25 Moses said, "Eat it today, for today is a Sabbath to the LORD; today you will not find it in the field. 26 Six days you shall gather it, but on the seventh day, which is a Sabbath, there will be none."

> On the sixth day they gathered twice as much bread for the Sabbath that God had commanded.

27 On the seventh day some of the people went out to gather, but they found none. 28 And the LORD said to Moses, "How long will you refuse to keep my commandments and my laws? 29 See! The LORD has given you the Sabbath; therefore on the sixth day he gives you bread for two days. Remain each of you in his place; let no one go out of his place on the seventh day." 30 So the people rested on the seventh day.

> Some did not listen to God's rule to follow the Sabbath.

Putting It All Together

> **31** Now the house of Israel called its name manna. It was like coriander seed, white, and the taste of it was like wafers made with honey. **32** Moses said, "This is what the LORD has commanded: 'Let an omer of it be kept throughout your generations, so that they may see the bread with which I fed you in the wilderness, when I brought you out of the land of Egypt.'" **33** And Moses said to Aaron, "Take a jar, and put an omer of manna in it, and place it before the LORD to be kept throughout your generations." **34** As the LORD commanded Moses, so Aaron placed it before the testimony to be kept. **35** The people of Israel ate the manna forty years, till they came to a habitable land. They ate the manna till they came to the border of the land of Canaan. **36** (An omer is the tenth part of an ephah.)

Israel called the bread manna. They kept some in a jar to remember God's faithfulness throughout all generations. They ate this manna for forty years in the wilderness.

Write out a one to two sentence summary. What is the main idea of this passage?

_____

_____

_____

Ashley's Insights

A month after being rescued from slavery in Egypt, Israel complains to God about being hungry in the wilderness; therefore, God miraculously provides for their needs by sending manna from heaven every morning. God tests them, commanding how much manna to gather (only enough for each day) and when to gather it (not on the Sabbath). Some Israelites fail the test and disobey God despite His daily provision.

THE EASY BIBLE STUDY METHOD

DIG DEEPER

Annotate the Passage

Annotate the same passage you paraphrased by identifying keywords and themes. Highlight or circle keywords and phrases, note the context of the passage, ask questions, define words, connect ideas, write out your prayers, write down your honest thoughts, and note God and His character.

Ashley's Insights

Exodus 16

1 They set out from Elim, and all the congregation of the people of Israel came to the wilderness of Sin, which is between Elim and Sinai, on the fifteenth day of the second month after they had departed from the land of Egypt. 2 And the whole congregation of the people of Israel grumbled against Moses and Aaron in the wilderness, 3 and the people of Israel said to them, "Would that we had died by the hand of the LORD in the land of Egypt, when we sat by the meat pots and ate bread to the full, for you have brought us out into this wilderness to kill this whole assembly with hunger."

Characters:
- The whole congregation of Israel
- Moses and Aaron
- The LORD

The people turning away from the LORD

150

Putting It All Together

4 Then the LORD said to Moses, "Behold, I am about to rain bread from heaven for you, and the people shall go out and gather a day's portion every day, that I may test them, whether they will walk in my law or not. **5** On the sixth day, when they prepare what they bring in, it will be twice as much as they gather daily." **6** So Moses and Aaron said to all the people of Israel, "At evening you shall know that it was the LORD who brought you out of the land of Egypt, **7** and in the morning you shall see the glory of the LORD, because he has heard your grumbling against the LORD. For what are we, that you grumble against us?" **8** And Moses said, "When the LORD gives you in the evening meat to eat and in the morning bread to the full, because the LORD has heard your grumbling that you grumble against him—what are we? Your grumbling is not against us but against the LORD."

9 Then Moses said to Aaron, "Say to the whole congregation of the people of Israel, 'Come near before the LORD, for he has heard your grumbling.'" **10** And as soon as Aaron spoke to the whole congregation

> God desired to test them to see if they would listen to Him and obey Him. It's God saying, "Do you love me? Do you trust me?" John 14:15: "If you love me, keep my commandments."

> 4x:
> "The Lord has heard your grumbling"

of the people of Israel, they looked toward the wil-

derness, and behold, the glory of the LORD appeared

in the cloud. **11** And the LORD said to Moses, **12** "I

have heard the grumbling of the people of Israel. Say

to them, 'At twilight you shall eat meat, and in the

morning you shall be filled with bread. Then you shall

know that I am the LORD your God.'"

13 In the evening quail came up and covered the

camp, and in the morning dew lay around the camp.

14 And when the dew had gone up, there was on the

face of the wilderness a fine, flake-like thing, fine as

frost on the ground. **15** When the people of Israel

saw it, they said to one another, "What is it?" For they

did not know what it was. And Moses said to them,

"It is the bread that the LORD has given you to eat. **16**

This is what the LORD has commanded: 'Gather of it,

each one of you, as much as he can eat. You shall each

take an omer, according to the number of the persons

that each of you has in his tent.'" **17** And the people of

Israel did so. They gathered, some more, some less.

18 But when they measured it with an omer, whoever

Putting It All Together

gathered much had nothing left over, and whoever gathered little had no lack. Each of them gathered as much as he could eat. **19** And Moses said to them, "Let no one leave any of it over till the morning." **20** But they did not listen to Moses. Some left part of it till the morning, and it bred worms and stank. And Moses was angry with them. **21** Morning by morning they gathered it, each as much as he could eat; but when the sun grew hot, it melted.

22 On the sixth day they gathered twice as much bread, two omers each. And when all the leaders of the congregation came and told Moses, **23** he said to them, "This is what the LORD has commanded: 'Tomorrow is a day of solemn rest, a holy Sabbath to the LORD; bake what you will bake and boil what you will boil, and all that is left over lay aside to be kept till the morning.'" **24** So they laid it aside till the morning, as Moses commanded them, and it did not stink, and there were no worms in it. **25** Moses said, "Eat it today, for today is a Sabbath to the LORD; today you will not find it in the field. **26** Six days you shall gather

THE EASY BIBLE STUDY METHOD

it, but on the seventh day, which is a Sabbath, there will be none."

27 On the seventh day some of the people went out to gather, but they found none. **28** And the LORD said to Moses, "How long will you refuse to keep my commandments and my laws? **29** See! The LORD has given you the Sabbath; therefore on the sixth day he gives you bread for two days. Remain each of you in his place; let no one go out of his place on the seventh day." **30** So the people rested on the seventh day.

31 Now the house of Israel called its name manna. It was like coriander seed, white, and the taste of it was like wafers made with honey. **32** Moses said, "This is what the LORD has commanded: 'Let an omer of it be kept throughout your generations, so that they may see the bread with which I fed you in the wilderness, when I brought you out of the land of Egypt.'" **33** And Moses said to Aaron, "Take a jar, and put an omer of manna in it, and place it before the LORD to be

Manna= "What is it?" The bread was not what they had expected it to be like.

154

Putting It All Together

> kept throughout your generations." **34** As the Lord **4** commanded Moses, so Aaron placed it before the testimony to be kept. **35** The people of Israel ate the manna forty years, till they came to a habitable land. They ate the manna till they came to the border of the land of Canaan. **36** (An omer is the tenth part of an ephah.)

Discover the Meaning

What did it mean for the original audience? Conclude in one sentence what the text meant for them in their day.

Ashley's Insights

Moses recounts the historical story of the Israelites complaining against God in the wilderness. God heard their complaints and provided for them manna from heaven every morning for forty years in the wilderness. God faithfully provided for His people, showing grace and steadfast love even when they themselves were stubborn, grumpy, and disobedient.

What does it mean for us today? What are the differences and similarities you share with the original audience?

THE EASY BIBLE STUDY METHOD

Differences:

Similarities:

Ashley's Insights

Differences:

- I am a woman living in the twenty-first century.
- I am a Christian living in the new covenant of Jesus' blood.
- I struggle to know what it's like to be wandering in a desert and feeling physically hungry.
- I do not have to follow the Old Testament laws as the Israelites did.

Similarities:

- The Lord rescued me from "slavery" to sin and death.
- I grumble and complain when I feel God isn't meeting my needs. God hears all my grumbling.
- I sometimes want to return to "slavery"—a time before I was saved because it seems better and easier.
- I may not physically have bread from God daily—but Jesus is my daily bread.
- God tests me, asking me, "Do you love Me? Do you trust Me?" My obedience shows my love for God.
- When I grumble and complain, it is ultimately against God Himself.
- I, too, struggle with disobedience, and God asks me to love Him and love people, and I fall short daily.
- Although I am not required to observe the Sabbath like the Israelites, I am still called to weekly rhythms of rest.

Putting It All Together

Conclude in one sentence what the text means for us today. Exodus 16 calls all believers to:

_____

_____

_____

Ashley's Insights

Exodus 16 calls all believers to consider the ways in which we believe God isn't meeting our needs and have turned to a spirit of complaining and grumbling. It challenges us to focus on our miracle-working God, who is faithful and does provide for our needs. Just as God provided for the Israelites' physical need for bread, God provides for our spiritual hunger through our daily bread, which is Jesus Christ Himself.

Commentaries

Look into a commentary or study Bible to add to your understanding of this text.

Commentary or study Bible:

_____

What new information did you learn about the meaning of Exodus 16?

_____

_____

_____

_____

_____

Ashley's Insights

The commentary I choose to study is the David Guzik *Enduring Word* commentary. The main thing that stood out to me was the connection to Jesus:

> This **manna**, this bread from heaven, is a powerful picture of Jesus Himself. After feeding the 5,000, some people wanted Him to keep feeding them with His miraculous power. They wanted Jesus to provide for them just as Israel was provided with manna in the wilderness. This is what Jesus said in reply:
>
> > "Most assuredly, I say to you, Moses did not give you the bread from heaven, but My Father gives you the true bread from heaven. For the bread of God is he who comes down from heaven and gives life to the world." (John 6:32–33)
>
> Jesus is the bread from heaven, and we must receive Him like Israel received the manna.
>
> - Aware of our need, hungry.
> - Each for himself, family by family.
> - Every day.
> - Humbly—perhaps even on our knees.
> - With gratitude, knowing we don't deserve it.
> - Eating it, taking the gift inside, to our innermost being.[15]

---

15. David Guzik, "Exodus 16—Bread from Heaven," *Enduring Word*, https://enduringword.com/bible-commentary/exodus-16/.

Putting It All Together

S—Seek God and His Character

STEP THREE: S – SEEK GOD AND HIS CHARACTER

Write out a list of who God is from the passage. **"God is _____"**

- Find explicit qualities and characteristics of God
  - Attributes plainly written in the text
- Find implicit qualities and characteristics of God
  - Look at the context clues, mainly actions, to find attributes not plainly stated

DIG DEEPER

Meditate on God's character through

- **Prayer:** Pray over the verses, focusing on praising God for who He is
- **Journaling:** Write down your own response to God's character through means of poetry, songwriting, a letter to God, or simple journal entry
- **Art:** Meditate on Scripture and have it inspire a watercolor, collage, sketching, etc.
- **Worship:** Sing songs that proclaim the attributes you read about

Write Out a List of Who God Is

Write out a list of God's explicit and implicit qualities and characteristics from the passage and explain how you came to each conclusion.

Explicit Qualities (only one found in this passage):

God is _____.

- _____

THE EASY BIBLE STUDY METHOD

Implicit Qualities (list at least five):

God is _____.

- _____

God is _____.

- _____

God is _____.

- _____

God is _____.

- _____

God is _____.

- _____

Are there any incorrect views of God from the Israelite people within this passage? If so, explain:

Incorrect view: God is _____.

- _____

Putting It All Together

Ashley's Insights

Explicit Qualities:

God **is LORD**

- *Exodus 16:12:* This is God's special name, Yahweh. This is what God calls Himself in Exodus 3:14 when He tells Moses, "I AM WHO I AM." This name signifies that God is eternal and self-existent. It also signifies His personal relationship with the Israelites, being a God who keeps covenant with them.

Implicit Qualities:

God **speaks**

- *Exodus 16:4:* God is not silent. He heard His people and responded.

God **hears**

- *Exodus 16:3, 7– 9, 12:* God heard their grumbling and took action to provide for His people.

God **tests people**

- *Exodus 16:4:* God tests the Israelites to see if they would obey His commands.

God **is a Savior**

- *Exodus 16:6:* God saved the Israelites from slavery in Egypt.

God **is glorious**

- *Exodus 16:10:* God's glory appeared in a cloud.

God **is personal**

- *Exodus 16:12:* God's desire is for the Israelites to know that He is the Lord their God—meaning He belongs to them personally.

God **is a miracle worker, and God provides**

- *Exodus 16:13–14:* God provides quail and manna for the people coming down from heaven during their entire time in the wilderness.

God **commands**

- *Exodus 16:6:* God gives rules for His people to follow.

God **gives the Sabbath**

- *Exodus 16:29:* God is the giver of the Sabbath.

Incorrect Views of God from the Israelites:

God is **unfaithful**

- How was their view of God wrong? They grumbled against God for taking them into the wilderness to "kill them" (Ex. 16:3, 8). They believed God to be unfaithful and did not trust in Him due to their immediate circumstances. We see from other parts of Scripture that God is faithful, full of steadfast love, and can be counted on (Ps. 100:5).

DIG DEEPER Meditate on God's character qualities found within this passage. Choose one of these activities:

- **Prayer:** Pray over the verses, focusing on praising God for who He is
- **Journaling:** Write down your response to God's character through means of poetry, songwriting, a letter to God, or simple journal entry
- **Art:** Meditate on Scripture and have it inspire a watercolor, collage, sketching, etc.
- **Worship:** Sing songs that proclaim the attributes you read about

Putting It All Together

Y—Yearn for a Heart Change and Deeper Intimacy with God

STEP FOUR: Y – YEARN FOR A HEART CHANGE AND DEEPER INTIMACY WITH GOD

Journaling questions for inward transformation of heart and mind

- In what ways is the Holy Spirit convicting me that my heart needs to look more like God's heart?
- How does my current way of thinking need to be challenged?
- What emotions am I feeling (e.g., fear, anxiety, bitterness) that need to be acknowledged and surrendered?
- Should I be more in awe of who God is and spend time simply praising Him for His character?
- How can a mindset shift, based on the text, change how I go about my day?

Journaling questions for outward application

- Does this text have explicit practical applications that I should follow?
- Does this text imply certain godly behaviors I should adopt as a believer?
- How can I look more like God? What practical steps can I take?
- Is this a passage that I should memorize and meditate on?

DIG DEEPER

- Create SMART goals to help you achieve your intended outcome.

Journal for Inward Transformation

Pick a journaling question for inward transformation that stands out to you. Take time to answer it.

Journaling Question:

Answer:

Ashley's Insights

Journaling Question:
How can a mindset shift, based on the text, change how I go about my day?

Answer:
I need to change my mindset to trust and believe rather than complain and grumble. My heart leans toward life's negatives, anxieties, and fears. But this passage shows me that God hears my grumbling and complaining, and I would instead prefer that I bring Him joy through gratitude and praise. I want to fight my fears and grumbles with trust, thanks, and praise to my God.

Putting It All Together

Journal for Outward Application

Pick a journaling question for outward application that stands out to you. Take time to answer it.

Journaling Question:

Answer:

> ### Ashley's Insights
>
> *Journaling Question:*
> Does this text imply certain godly behaviors I should adopt as a believer?
>
> *Answer:*
> I see many godly behaviors I can apply to my life from this text:
> - Trust in God's faithfulness rather than grumble and complain against Him
> - Show love to God through obedience to His ways
> - Honor the Lord's Sabbath day by resting and looking to Him
> - Remember how He has saved me, and know He is my God and my Savior
>
> Dear Lord, I see in this passage many ways I need to grow and change. I see how my heart needs to change. I believe You are good and faithful,

165

but I struggle with unbelief too. Help my unbelief. Please, Holy Spirit, convict me when I turn to grumbling and complaining. Lord, You are my provider and will always remain faithful to me. Thank You for all the ways You have already provided for me—especially through Jesus, my daily bread. Let my heart sing of Your praises, and thank You for all You have done for me. I love You, Lord. Help me to love You and trust You more.

Conclusion

From Ashley

I want to leave you with a few final thoughts and actions so you can practically apply the EASY Bible Study Method to your life. We created this method to help you incorporate Bible study into your everyday routine. The Bible can't transform you if it collects dust on your bookshelf or nightstand. The beauty of Scripture comes through meeting God in every story, every page, and every word of His magnificent, Spirit-inspired Word.

My biggest advice to you is to show up every day. It may be hard at first. It might not feel easy. You may struggle to grasp God's words. It will take time for you to feel confident in your knowledge of the story of the Bible and each unique book within God's Word. Be like a child—soak up Scripture like a sponge. Ask questions. Learn new words, locations, and themes. Read books and commentaries to help you along the way. Study Scripture with friends. Don't throw in the towel when you feel frustrated or confused or when you skip a few days of reading. Don't beat yourself up if you get behind. Show up—even when you're tired or don't feel like it, even when you only want to scroll through social media or binge your favorite Netflix show.

Use this method to help you study Scripture daily. The more you immerse yourself in Scripture, the easier studying and reading the Bible will become. But, friend, you must put in the time, effort, and hard work. You must be patient as you learn and grow. Trust me when I say this: Immersing yourself in God's Word is one of the best investments of your time you will ever make. The more you put in, the more you will get out—and soon enough, studying the Bible will come naturally and easily to you through the help and power of the Holy Spirit!

What You Will Learn

In this chapter, you will learn how to incorporate the EASY Bible Study Method into your life. Here are the questions you'll be given answers to:

- When and where will I study?
- Where in the Bible will I start?
- Who will I study with?

When and Where to Study

Let's start with when and where you will be studying the Bible. If your goal is to learn how to study the Bible and be consistent in your Scripture reading, then specific, measurable goals can help you progress.

When is the best time for you to study the Bible? I highly encourage you to commit to reading the Bible daily and at the same time every day. This consistency will create a habit within your routine, making it more likely for you to achieve your goal of learning how to study the Bible. Once the habit is formed, you won't have to think about creating a space for Bible study—it will come naturally.

Are you a morning person or a night person? I usually encourage my mentees to choose a time early in the morning, right after they wake up, or at night, right before going to bed. I'm a morning person, so I enjoy making a cup of coffee and opening my Bible in the stillness of the morning before the day gets crazy and hectic. But I also remember a season where doing my Bible study at night was better for me because I was already waking up early for school and had more time before bed. Or perhaps mornings and evenings don't work for you. Maybe a lunch hour is better. Any time of your day that you can carve out fifteen to twenty minutes of stillness will work great. Choose the best time for you and commit to it.

168

I recently received a comment from one of our followers, who is a mom of four kids. She dedicates time every morning to be with God, studying His Word. She goes into her bedroom with the door shut for half an hour every morning. Her children know this is her time for quiet and peace with the Lord (and many mornings, a tiny hand comes knocking at her door when the half hour is up). Although it is hard to carve out this time with four kids, she has made it a priority in her life.

Where is it best for you to study the Bible? Along with committing to a time, it is also good to commit to a place. For me, it's in my living room on my couch. I keep my Bible and notebook on the coffee table so I can easily pick them up and study every morning. I tend to be messy, so I make sure my environment is clean and picked up before studying. This helps my mind feel uncluttered and ready for Bible study. Do you have a quiet and clean environment to study God's Word?

And since we are on the topic of a focused mind, I would also encourage you to have a spot in your journal to write down all the urgent thoughts that come up when doing Bible study, such as *I need to do laundry today*, or *I forgot to text Sarah back and need to text her back now before it's too late*. Now is no time to worry about laundry or texting Sarah back. Write these thoughts in the "brain dump" section of a notebook, and then return to that list after your Bible reading time.

If you are using your phone for Bible study, make sure you set it on Do Not Disturb. Resist the urge to scroll through social media during the dull moments. If you feel like certain apps are too distracting, you can always delete them during your quiet time and redownload them afterward. If you are anything like me, you may struggle with squirrel brain. I am easily distracted. So, I usually choose to do my Bible study with a physical copy of the Bible and a notebook rather than on my phone. But I do occasionally use my phone for online research, commentaries, or to look up any Bible-related questions I may have.

TAKE ACTION Commit to when and where you will consistently be studying your Bible.

When:

Where:

Where in the Bible to Start

Perhaps the biggest question I get in my ministry is: *Where should I start reading the Bible?* This is such a valid question because the Bible is huge! It has sixty-six books, 1,189 chapters, two testaments, and loads of stories and genres to choose from. Most people jump around when reading Scripture, which can make it confusing when first trying to understand it. So, where do you start?

The Bible is a unique book because you can begin reading it in many different places:

- You can start at the beginning and **read it through from Genesis to Revelation.** It's a big task but possible!
- You can choose **a specific book** to focus on. If you are new to reading the Bible, I would suggest starting with the book of John. Since Jesus is central to the entire Bible and our faith, I think reading **John would be a great place to begin** so that you can learn more about Jesus and the gospel and see your faith and belief grow.
- You can choose a specific **chapter** to read, like a psalm. Sometimes, it's nice to focus on one particular chapter of the Bible, and I love to read individual psalms.
- Or, you can choose a specific **verse** to focus on, such as a proverb, or a verse that really stands out to you, such as John 3:16.

TAKE ACTION

What in the Bible will you commit to reading?

Who to Study With

Last, who will you be studying with? Will you go solo, study with a friend or mentor, or use it in your small group?

Solo

Studying the Bible solo is a great choice for those who want some one-on-one time with Jesus and will use the EASY Bible Study Method in their personal quiet time.

With a Friend or Mentor

I highly recommend doing this method with a friend or mentor. If you commit to doing this with someone, you will be able to hold each other accountable. You can share with each other what you have been learning. Bible study can be richer when we do it with others.

You can go through the method together at the same time, or you can go through the method individually and then come together to go over what you learned and any insights you had.

With a Small Group

You can also use the method with a church small group or any group of people who desire to learn how to study the Bible. Use this book as a guide, and feel free to use the discussion questions at the end of each chapter.

TAKE ACTION

If you are choosing to study with someone, write their name (or names) here:

_____

_____

_____

Friend, that is it. We have given you all the tools you will need to start studying the Bible! Hopefully, now you have a plan for when and where you will study, what part of the Bible you will explore, and who you will study with. Remember, this is just the beginning of the journey. There will be moments of confusion and frustration, but over time, you will grow to become a confident student of God's Word!

Your dedication to learning how to read the Bible will be an investment that will one day reap a harvest of much fruit. God's Word is eternal, unchanging, and relevant to every stage of your life. Know that the one who meditates on it is blessed (Ps. 1). The Bible will touch every part of your heart, resonate with your story in ways you never imagined, and fill you with the hope and courage to persevere in this life until He takes you home.

A Note to Mentors

From Mentor Mama Ellen

If you are in the process of mentoring, my daughters and I highly recommend that you use this book as a resource to shepherd your mentee in their Bible reading journey. We have each walked alongside women through mentoring and have found that the most valuable gifts you can give are your patience and tools to help them study their Bible. This book will help your mentee ultimately learn to study her Bible independently and correctly. It will also provide you with all the necessary teaching (yay!), discussion questions, and exercises to do together.

Here are some tips for walking through this book with your mentee:

- Assign chapters with advance notice to your mentee so you can do the reading separately if that works best for them. If your mentee would do better reading through the chapters together, you can do that instead. Assess what may work best for them. Feel free to ask them their preference.

- You must become familiar with each aspect of the EASY Bible Study Method *before* leading your mentee through it. This will ensure that you are prepared to guide them through each chapter effectively and answer any questions they may have.

- Communicate to your mentee that the Bible is both simple and profound. Through the power of the Holy Spirit, they will gain wisdom (2 Tim. 3:15) and be steadily challenged. Encourage them to be open to growth and learning, even if they need more time to grasp everything. It's a process.

- Encourage them to write down their questions so they can ask you about them. Remind them that there are no "stupid" questions and that you are a safe place to ask them. Do not worry if you don't know all the answers either; you can always tell your mentee you aren't sure about the answer and ask a pastor or seek a commentary for help.

- Before you start the Bible study, pray together for God to be present and for your hearts to be opened to His words.

- Each chapter has Take Action sections that you and your mentee can do together (or if you choose to do them separately, you can later go over your answers together). The Take Action sections mainly focus on studying John 6:1–15.

- Doing The EASY Bible Study Method together is essential because it allows your mentee to practice doing Bible study with the help of their mentor rather than trying to learn how to do it alone.

- At the end of each chapter are discussion questions you and your mentee can discuss.

- Always close your time with your mentee by asking how you can pray for them. This question will help them ponder what is happening in their life and encourage them to open up to you. The bond between you and your mentee will grow stronger and stronger as time goes on, and they will see that you are faithful to be there for them in Bible study and their personal life.

As we wrap up this book, I want to encourage you in your mentoring by sharing my story. I worked in corporate America for thirteen years after college. When our oldest, Andrew, entered kindergarten, I felt the urgency of getting him into a church with a thriving kids' program, yet ironically, I was not a believer. One day, while playing with Andrew at the park, a neighbor told me about his church and encouraged my husband and me to check it out, which we quickly did. God spoke through the pastor in a mighty way, and before I knew it, I had accepted Christ as my personal Savior while attending their Grace 101 class.

Simultaneously, I struggled with long commutes and workdays and felt cheated that I could only spend a couple of hours with my children after work before they went to bed. After seeking professional counseling, my husband and I decided that I would stay home with the kids for "a while." This little while quickly turned into a decade before I would once again return to the workforce.

That step from a full-time management role in corporate America to being a stay-at-home mom was a joyful yet challenging transition. I had no friends in this new world until I heard about the MOMS (Making Our Mothering Significant) ministry one Sunday morning at church. Those interested would head to a table in the lobby for more information. I was greeted by smiling faces who responded to my felt need for friendship, but God knew my greater need was to know Him more. Before long, I began attending MOMS, where I was fed scriptural truths and fostered friendships, ultimately enriching my family. Not only did the yearly Bible studies hold me accountable to learning God's Word, but equally important, I was poured into every year by a mentor. Witnessing these mentors who knew their Bibles forward and backward and called upon Scripture from memory was a revolutionary experience for me.

One particular mentor, Melinda, captured my heart. I'll never forget one Sunday afternoon when she invited our small group for a homemade dinner. As I entered her home, the aroma of baked Italian stuffed pasta shells and fresh garlic bread wafted through the air. Sitting snug up against the person next to me in her tiny dining room, I cherished her love for us that she would go to such great lengths to prepare a meal and serve a group of ten tired and weary moms.

Her words were always wise each week, backed by biblical truths. She also took the time to meet with me individually, curious and fully present, and our visits were never absent of laughter. She has prayed for me and helped guide me in various church leadership roles I have had throughout the years. It was this experience with Melinda and several others that God used to put mentoring on my heart now and for years to come.

Not only can you make a life-changing impact on the person you are mentoring, but you are also equipping your mentee to one day pass along what she has learned to mentor someone else. If you embark on this mentoring journey, it will be one of the most rewarding experiences you will encounter in your Christian walk.

So, ask a mentee to join you on this adventure, or find a mentor you admire, and get started!

APPENDIX A

John 6:1–15

Jesus Feeds the Five Thousand

1 After this Jesus went away to the other side of the Sea of Galilee, which is the Sea of Tiberias. **2** And a large crowd was following him, because they saw the signs that he was doing on the sick. **3** Jesus went up on the mountain, and there he sat down with his disciples. **4** Now the Passover, the feast of the Jews, was at hand. **5** Lifting up his eyes, then, and seeing that a large crowd was coming toward him, Jesus said to Philip, "Where are we to buy bread, so that these people may eat?" **6** He said this to test him, for he himself knew what he would do. **7** Philip answered him, "Two hundred denarii worth of bread would not be enough for each of them to get a little." **8** One of his disciples, Andrew, Simon Peter's brother, said to him, **9** "There is a boy here who has five barley loaves and two fish, but what are they for so many?" **10** Jesus said, "Have the people sit down." Now there was much grass in the place. So the men sat down, about five thousand in number. **11** Jesus then took the loaves, and when he had given thanks, he distributed them to those who were seated. So also the fish, as much as they wanted. **12** And when they had eaten their fill, he told his disciples, "Gather up the leftover fragments, that nothing may be lost." **13** So they gathered them up and filled twelve baskets with fragments from the five barley loaves left by those who had eaten. **14** When the people saw the sign that he had done, they said, "This is indeed the Prophet who is to come into the world!" **15** Perceiving then that they were about to come and take him by force to make him king, Jesus withdrew again to the mountain by himself.

APPENDIX B

Recommended Resources

Commentaries
- NIV Application Commentaries
- *The Wiersbe Bible Commentary* (Old Testament and New Testament)
- Grant R. Osborne Commentaries
- *The Moody Bible Commentary*
- D. A. Carson Commentaries
- *The Wycliffe Bible Commentary*

Study Bibles
- *ESV Study Bible* by ESV Bibles
- *NIV Cultural Backgrounds Study Bible* by Zondervan
- *NIV Life Application Study Bible* by Zondervan
- *NLT Life Application Study Bible* by Tyndale
- *ESV The Hebrew-Greek Key Word Study Bible* by AMG Publishers
- *NIV Archaeological Study Bible* by Zondervan

Bible Dictionaries
- *Nelson's Illustrated Bible Dictionary* by Ronald F. Youngblood
- *The Ultimate Bible Dictionary* by Holman Bible Publishers

Book Recommendations

- Learn more about the Trinity:
  - *Delighting in the Trinity* by Michael Reeves
- Learn more about the genres of the Bible:
  - *Literarily: How Understanding Bible Genres Transforms Bible Study* by Kristie Anyabwile

Resources

Scan for a downloadable PDF of *The EASY Bible Study Method* resource links or go to:

coffeeandbibletime.com/easy-bible-study-method-links/

APPENDIX C

EASY Bible Study Method Guides

STEP ONE: E – ENTER INTO THE STORY

- **Pray** before reading
- **Read** the text slowly and thoughtfully
- **Determine** the context
  - Where does this fit in the storyline of the Bible?
  - Who was the original author?
  - Who was the original audience and what were they going through?
- **Put** yourself in the story
- **Ask** good questions

DIG DEEPER

- Read the text in different translations: ESV, NLT, NIV, NKJV
- When was this written? What was the date? What major events were going on during this time?
- Are there any historical or cultural things, customs, locations, or elements within the text that could be researched more in order to understand the meaning?
- What is the surrounding context of the verse or passage you are studying?
- What is the literary genre of this text and how does that add to the meaning of the passage?

Appendix C

STEP TWO: A – ASSESS THE MAIN IDEA

Paraphrase the passage in your own words.

- Break up the text into chunks for summarizing into bite-size pieces and then write out a 1–2 sentence paraphrase.
- Ask yourself: What is the main idea of this passage?

DIG DEEPER

- Annotate the passage (identifying keywords and themes).
  - Highlight or circle keywords and phrases, make notes of the context of the passage, ask questions, define words, connect ideas, write out your prayers, write down your honest thoughts, note God and His character.
- Discover the meaning of the passage:
  - What did it mean for the original audience? Conclude in one sentence what the text meant for them in their day.
  - What does it mean for us today? What are the differences and similarities you share with the original audience? Conclude in one sentence what the text means for us today.
- Seek help from commentaries if necessary.

Resources

Scan for a downloadable PDF of *The EASY Bible Study Method* resource links or go to:

coffeeandbibletime.com/easy-bible-study-method-links/

THE EASY BIBLE STUDY METHOD

STEP THREE: S – SEEK GOD AND HIS CHARACTER

Write out a list of who God is from the passage. **"God is _____"**

- Find explicit qualities and characteristics of God
  - Attributes plainly written in the text
- Find implicit qualities and characteristics of God
  - Look at the context clues, mainly actions, to find attributes not plainly stated

DIG DEEPER

Meditate on God's character through

- **Prayer:** Pray over the verses, focusing on praising God for who He is

- **Journaling:** Write down your own response to God's character through means of poetry, songwriting, a letter to God, or simple journal entry

- **Art:** Meditate on Scripture and have it inspire a watercolor, collage, sketching, etc.

- **Worship:** Sing songs that proclaim the attributes you read about

Appendix C

STEP FOUR: Y – YEARN FOR A HEART CHANGE AND DEEPER INTIMACY WITH GOD

Journaling questions for inward transformation of heart and mind

- In what ways is the Holy Spirit convicting me that my heart needs to look more like God's heart?
- How does my current way of thinking need tobe challenged?
- What emotions am I feeling (e.g., fear, anxiety, bitterness) that need to be acknowledged and surrendered?
- Should I be more in awe of who God is and spend time simply praising Him for His character?
- How can a mindset shift, based on the text, change how I go about my day?

Journaling questions for outward application

- Does this text have explicit practical applications that I should follow?
- Does this text imply certain godly behaviors I should adopt as a believer?
- How can I look more like God? What practical steps can I take?
- Is this a passage that I should memorize and meditate on?

DIG DEEPER

- Create SMART goals to help you achieve your intended outcome.

THE EASY BIBLE STUDY METHOD

Date: _____   Bible Passage: _____

Step One:
E
ENTER THE STORY

- **Pray** before reading
- **Read** the text slowly and throughtfully
- **Determine** the context
  - Where does this fit in the storyline of the Bible?
  - Who was the original author?
  - Who was the original audience and what were they going through?
- **Put** yourself in the story
- **Ask** good questions

Step Two:
A
ASSESS THE MAIN IDEA

- **Paraphrase** the passage in your own words:
  - Break up the text summarizing into bite-size pieces
  - Write out a 1–2 sentence summary of the main idea of this passage

Step Three:
S
SEEK GOD & HIS CHARACTER

Write out a list of who God is from the passage
"God is: _____"
- Find explicit qualities and characteristics of God
  - Attributes plainly written in the text
- Find implicit qualities and characteristics of God
  - Look at context clues, mainly actions, to find attributes not plainly stated

Step Four:
Y
YEARN FOR A HEART CHANGE

Journaling question for inward transformation of heart and mind
- In what ways is the Holy Spirit convicting me that my heart needs to look more like God's heart?

Journaling question for outward application
- How can I look more like God? What practical steps can I take?

APPENDIX D

Map

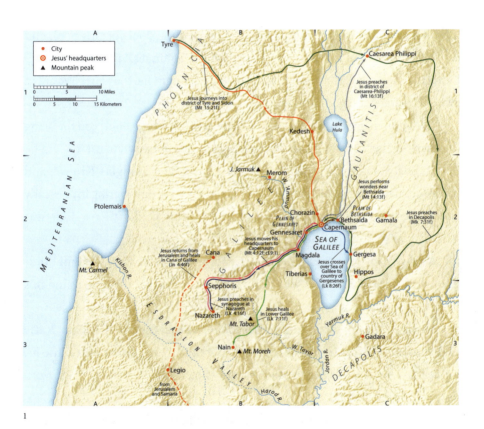

---

1. Barry J. Beitzel, *The Moody Bible Atlas* (Moody Publishers: Chicago, 2025), 263.

Acknowledgments

All glory to God—He is the One who opened the door for this book and brought us this far! Like King David said in 2 Samuel 7:18, "Who am I, O Lord God, and what is my house, that you have brought me thus far?" We are in awe of His grace and goodness.

To our amazing **Coffee and Bible Time community**—thank you for being the heartbeat behind this book. Your support means the world to us!

To our wonderful husbands, **Johnny Armijo** and **Douglas Krause**, and to Taylor's fiancé, **Isaac Mitchelle**—thank you for your unwavering love, steady encouragement, and constant belief in us. We truly couldn't have done this without you!

A huge thank-you to **Ellen's Grace Group**—Lisa McEachin, Viviani Lindgren,** and **Kristin Bos**—for your thoughtful feedback and helping refine this book with so much care.

To our dear former mentors—**Melinda Averbeck, Carissa Erickson, Katie O'Brien,** and **Allison Thomas**—thank you for the way you once poured into us, modeling what it looks like to follow Jesus wholeheartedly and love His Word deeply. We're so grateful.

Thank you to **Moody Bible Institute** for shaping us with a rich foundation in God's Word. Special thanks to **Dr. Ronald Sauer, Dr. James Coakley, Dr. Steven Sanchez**, and **Dr. Pamela MacRae**—your teaching left a lasting impact. And to **Dr. Bradley Baurain**, thank you for being the first to believe in Ashley's writing dreams!

Acknowledgments

To our church families at **Village Church of Gurnee** and **Calvary Church**, and sweet friends like **Mollie Hansen, Rachel Goodall,** and **Ellie Powers**—thank you for your constant encouragement and prayers.

Endless gratitude to our incredible publishing team: **Judy Dunagan** (you believed in us before college!), **Erin Davis, Ashleigh Slater, Connor Sterchi, Hope Francis, Christianne Debysingh**, and **Janis Backing**—you made this dream a reality. And to **Sam Choy**, thank you for seeing potential in us from the very beginning.

Our hearts are full. Thank you, thank you, thank you!

Connect with us!

Coffee AND Bible Time

Coffee and Bible Time is a vibrant Christian **YouTube channel** and **podcast** where sisters Ashley and Taylor and their Mentor Mama, Ellen, post weekly to encourage and equip people to delight in God's Word and thrive in Christian living!

coffeeandbibletime.com

Join thousands using our resources:

- Free downloadables
- Faith-based blog
- Online shop featuring **#1 selling prayer journal**
- In-Depth Bible Study Academy
- Online community
- Uplifting newsletter
- Inspirational Instagram

MOODY PUBLISHERS
WOMEN
BIBLE STUDIES

REFRESHINGLY DEEP BIBLE STUDIES TO DWELL & DELIGHT IN GOD'S WORD

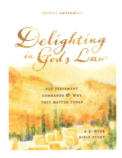
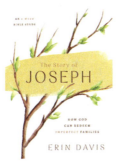

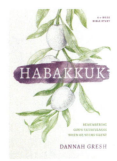
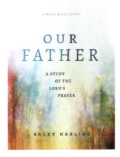
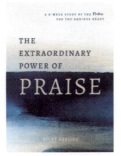

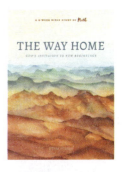
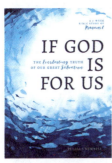
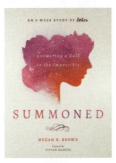

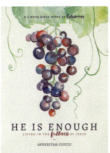
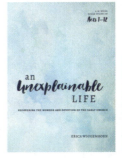
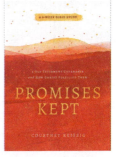

Find yours at: MoodyPublishersWomen.com